Visual Cultures

Visual Cultures

Edited by James Elkins

intellect Bristol, UK / Chicago, USA

First published in the UK in 2010 by Intellect,
The Mill, Parnall Road, Fishponds, Bristol, BS16 3JG, UK

First published in the USA in 2010 by Intellect, The University of Chicago Press,
1427 E. 60th Street, Chicago, IL 60637, USA

A catalogue record for this book is available from the British Library.

Cover design: Holly Rose
Copy-editor: Lesley Williams
Typesetting: John Teehan

ISBN 978-1-84150-307-3

Printed and bound in Great Britain by 4edge Ltd, Hockley. www.4edge.co.uk

FSC Mixed Sources
SA-COC-001695
FSC © 1996 FSC A.C.

Contents

Introduction 1

Slovenia: Visuality and Literarity In Slovene Culture 7
    Andrej Smrekar

Japan: Lost In Translation, or *Nothing* To See but Everything 27
    Sunil Manghani

Ireland: Words Upon the Windowpane: Image, Text, and Irish Culture 43
    Luke Gibbons

Poland: A Visually-Oriented Literary Culture? 57
    Kris Van Heuckelom

China: Verbal Above Visual: A Chinese Perspective 71
    Ding Ning

Russia: To Read, To Look: Teaching Visual Studies In Moscow 83
    Viktoria Musvik

Critical Response 97
    Esther Sánchez-Pardo

Contributors 111

INTRODUCTION

W hy gather a set of essays about concepts of the visual in different nations? Because the nation, as a site for the study of visuality, has been eclipsed by two complementary kinds of studies: those that focus on transnational, international, and global culture; and those that concentrate on local or regional culture.

Scholarship on visuality in global culture is moving rapidly, with new and forthcoming studies by many scholars—David Summers, Whitney Davis, Hans Belting, Iftikhar Dadi, Partha Mitter, Thomas DaCosta Kaufmann, and others (Elkins, et al., 2009; see also van Damme, et al., 2008). On the other hand, there is also a rapidly growing literature on visuality and literacy in particular places. There are studies, for example, of the "visual cultures" of individual cities such as Los Angeles and of particular cultures and cultural practices such as contemporary Aboriginal art (Isé 1998; Walsh 2000). In comparison there are relatively few studies of visuality or visual culture in nations. The existing scholarship tends to focus on particular periods in the history of nations, employing the vocabulary of visual studies to articulate practices that are particular to moments in the nations' histories.[1]

This bifurcated literature is, in part, a result of the pressure of political theory, which drives outward, toward issues of empire and transnationalism, or inward, toward issues of the everyday, the local, and the regional. Theorists such as Saskia Sassen, Immanuel Wallerstein, Dipesh Chakrabarty, Anthony King, Pascale Casanova, and Arjun Appadurai have transformed the discourse on the global and the local culture, and in the process the nation has become more a locus of theoretical discussion than of substantive study. In addition, the nation has long been the focus, and even the defining purpose, of traditional art history. As Hans Belting and others have shown, early- and mid-twentieth-century *Kunstgeschichte* was both openly and inadvertently nationalist, and the amalgamated and increasingly global discipline of art history retains many elements of those earlier discourses (Belting 1998). In the past few decades, the many developments that have led away from traditional art history—including varieties of visual studies and *Bildwissenschaft* as well as postcolonial studies, area studies, and decolonial studies—have also led away from studies that concentrate on national themes.

The six histories of ideas about visuality and literacy in this book are examples of what can be said about visuality and valuations of the visual in relation to national histories. These essays are primarily historical and not theoretical: they are replete with exact examples set in precise historical contexts, responding to specific politics and expressed in local languages. It is my hope that these histories can suggest forms of the dialectic relation between values accorded to language and to visuality that are not immediately present in current theorizations. The extensive discussions in the book *Art and Globalization* (Elkins, et al., 2009) work to problematize the local and the global culture, but they do not contribute directly to a rethinking of what can be said about the visual on a national scale. That book is as large as this one is small—*Art and Globalization* (Elkins, et al., 2009) includes fifty or sixty scholars from about forty countries—and this book was begun and largely completed before *Art and Globalization* (Elkins, et al., 2009). Yet this book can be read as a response to *Art and Globalization* (Elkins, et al., 2009) because it addresses a hiatus in conceptualization, where thinking about the national situation has moved into critical theory, whereas thinking about both global art and local practices of art have remained fruitful areas for historically specific work. (On the other hand, the historical inquiries in this book are not substitutes for the critical theory that informs current discourse: the brevity of this book does not condense or even address the crucial ongoing efforts to conceptualize the local, the regional, the transnational, the global, and the national culture.)

There is also the question of the generalization of western critical theory. For the most part, theorizations of collective identity, nationality, colonialism and postcolonialism, hybridity, and marginality have drawn on historiographic concepts and interpretive strategies formulated within western Europe and North America, even when they have taken as their subjects nations and cultures outside the West (Elkins 2003, pp. 110–120).[2] The same is true of studies of "scopic regimes," ocularcentrism, and the gaze. It can sometimes feel as if theorizations of the ocularcentric ideology, perspectival naturalism, "panoptical social surveillance," and other such concepts have reached a limit defined by their geographic and historical specificity.[3] Word and image studies, too, have reached a point where an enormous amount of literature on individual objects—much of it produced in and around the International Association of Word and Image Studies—relies on a relatively small number of theorizations, most of them developed in response to themes that are taken to be general throughout the postclassical West. These limits have not been invisible; in *Art and Globalization* (Elkins, et al., 2009), for example, García Canclini and others suggest that hybridization should be complemented by terms that are better suited for other parts of the world, such as South America. But hybridization remains to develop some of them in national contexts—*Art and Globalization* (Elkins, et al., 2009) issues several calls for rethinking hybridization but that work is not done in the book itself.

Readers should find a wealth of new ideas to contemplate in these essays. Andrej Smrekar's lucid summary of Slovene attitudes to the visual includes the fundamental point that Slovene national identity was forged by "men of letters" and "oriented predominantly toward literarity"—and yet, unexpectedly, the emergence of Slovenia was articulated best by visual objects. The occult reappearance of the visual through the literary is a recurrent theme in these essays. Kris Van Heuckelom's study of Polish literary and visual culture picks out several moments when literary culture seemed compelled to defend its purity, such as Julian Klaczko's claim that "As Slavs, we are and can be only masters of the Word!" and the poet Witold Gombrowicz's call for Poles to stop prostrating themselves before French painting. Those protests articulate a defensive fear, the inevitable companion of an unexpressed desire. The play of an articulate, publicly acceptable iconophobia and a private, pervasive iconophilia is another theme shared by several of these essays. Ding Ning's essay on China is a succinct survey of two thousand years of determinedly literary educational traditions, and it ends with only a faint hint—a hope—that university education in China might become more centered on images. Ning's pessimism—if that is what it is—is a tonic to the exuberant celebrations of visual culture that mark western publications on visual culture. We have to remember that we—that is, "we" in North America and Anglophone Europe, where this book is likely to be read—are a tiny minority, despite the apparent preeminence of visual media in global capitalist culture. No less important, we need to keep in mind that the current infatuation with visuality is arguably a trait of western Modernism and therefore a new and probably ephemeral interest in the history of culture. Viktoria Musvik's very honest essay—she is courageous in the claims she allows herself to make about Russian literacy and senses of the visual—is a tonic in this regard.

The pervasiveness of western European and North American theories of visuality's history has made it difficult to discern some workings of the visual and the literary outside the western compass. That problem is itself the subject of Sunil Manghani's meditation on Japan in Chapter 2. Manghani is an outsider to Japan, and his essay often turns on other people's meditations on their outsideness. (The movie *Lost in Translation* [Coppola 2003] plays as big a role in his essay as Roland Barthes's *Empire of Signs* [1983].) It is possible that for some Japanese readers, Manghani's essay may seem a bit forced, or even naff. But that lack of fluency is not a trait to be expunged: As Manghani knows, it is the condition of observation itself, in its perpetual partial exile. (Manghani is as sensitive and an eloquent observer of this form of alienation as any I know.) Irremediable partial alienation is a commonplace of postcolonial literature and existential philosophy; however, in the context of this book, it is a reminder of its opposite—the settled and confident voice of the native speaker and what such a voice can say.

In her critical meditation at the end of this book, Esther Sánchez-Pardo implicitly criticizes some authors for assuming that there can be such a thing as a history of the visuality or literacy of any given nation, outside the philosophic and political conditions that gave rise to the ideas of literacy and visuality. She is skeptical of the idea of writing about national histories and about writing histories about these subjects as if they could be distinguished from the histories that have given rise to our awareness of them. Her Critical Response is an apt summary of the reasons one might be—should be—skeptical of a book like this one. And yet the voices she summons emerge from western European and North American senses of the visual and the literary. What a wonderful thing to learn that Gombrowicz called for the Poles to remain faithful to their literacy and not to fall for French visuality: "Prostrate yourselves before painting, like the French? . . . it is not in our nature because our traditions are different."

*

This book began as the first day of a conference called "Visual Literacy." The idea was to begin the conference with strong, clear histories of specific national contexts, to give participants on the succeeding days something new against which to push, on which to test their ideas. As it turned out, on the next day most speakers chose not to engage the new material but to work on visual literacy using existing interpretive sources. So it is fortuitous that my editors decided to split the conference into several books.[4] That decision has given this book a clear and consistent purpose that is, perhaps, unusual in edited volumes, and it would have been a little lost in a larger book on the full conference.

I owe most to the people who helped arrange the conference, which took place at University College Cork, Ireland: Gerard Wrixon, then president of the university, who was largely responsible for setting up the History of Art initiative and securing the funds that made the conference possible; Veronica Fraser, the excellent administrator for History of Art; James Cronin, who managed everything from room bookings to audiovisual problems; and my colleagues at the university, Flavio Boggi, Simon Knowles, and Sabine Kriebel. Students helped as well, especially Enda Horgan and John Paul McMahon. I left the position in Ireland in summer 2006 and was sad to do so.

References

Barthes, Roland (1983), *Empire of Signs*. Translated from French by Richard Howard. New York: Hill and Wang.

Belting, Hans (1998), *The Germans and Their Art: A Troublesome Relationship*, Translated from German by Scott Kleager. New Haven: Yale University Press.

Collier, Delina (2008a), "The Reception of 'Nationalist' Art: A Response," *African Arts*, 41 (4) p. 8.

Collier, Delinda, (2008b), "Trans/nationalism in Angola," *African Arts*, 41, (3) pp. 10–11.

Coppola, Sofia (2003), *Lost in Translation*, Tokyo: Elemental Films.

Elkins, James (2003), *Visual Studies: A Skeptical Introduction*, New York: Routledge.

Elkins, James. ed. (2007a), *Visual Literacy*, New York: Routledge.

Elkins, James. ed. (2007b), *Visual Practices Across the University*, Munich: Wilhelm Fink Verlag.

Elkins, James, Valiavicharska, Zhivka, & Kim, Alice eds. (2009), *Art and Globalization*, University Park: Penn State Press.

Haakenson, Thomas Odell (2006) "Grotesque visions: art, science, and visual culture in early twentieth-century Germany," PhD dissertation, Twin Cities: University of Minnesota.

Isé, Claudine Anne Marie (1998), "'Visual culture and the political aesthetics of postmodern urbanism in Los Angeles," PhD dissertation, Los Angeles: University of Southern California.

Manghani, Sunil, Piper, Adrian, & Simons, Jon eds., General introduction to their readers. In S. Manghani, A. Piper, & J. Simons eds. (2006), *Images: A Reader*. Thousand Oaks: Sage, p. 6.

van Damme, Wilfried & Zijlmans, Kitty eds. (2008), *World Art Studies*, Leiden: Valiz.

van Den Berg, Dirk J. (2004), "What is an image and what is image power?" *Image and Narrative*, 4 (8) http://www.imageandnarrative.be/issue08/dirkvandenbergh.htm.

Walsh, Andrea Naomi (2000), "Contemporary Aboriginal art texts: intersections of visual culture," PhD dissertation, Toronto: York University.

Zitzewitz, Karin (2006), "The aesthetics of Secularism: Modernist art and visual culture in India," PhD dissertation, New York: Columbia University.

Endnotes

1. See, among many examples, Zitzewitz (2006), Haakenson (2006), and the interesting discussion of Angolan national visual culture in Collier (2008b, a).

2. This is argued, in reference to Gayatri Spivak and Slavoj Žižek in Elkins (2003, pp. 110–120).

3. I am quoting here from a summary of the ideas in Van Den Berg (2004), summarized by Manghani, et al., (2006). I choose this particular citation to suggest that the ideas are ubiquitous (because Van Den Berg is just summarizing the work of many others) and still very useful (because Manghani is one of the authors in this book).

4. The succeeding days of the conference are published in Elkins (2007a). The book was originally supposed to also contain an exhibition that was held at the same time as the conference, which is published in Elkins (2007b).

Visuality and Literarity In Slovene Culture

Andrej Smrekar

I cannot assess from this standpoint whether the relationship between literarity and visuality in Slovene cultural history carries any outstanding peculiarities. If you ask a Slovene what constituted his identity, the answer would be unequivocal: language, writing, the book, Protestantism, and France Prešeren (1800–1849), whose verses were adopted for our modern anthem a century and a half later.[1] At the accession to the European Union in May 2004, the National and University Library showed four of our earliest manuscripts—fragments of Slovene language between the tenth and fifteenth centuries—under the title "The Birth Certificate of Slovene Culture" (National and University Library 2004). They were the objects of a national pilgrimage. Slovene cultural history has been burdened by the heritage of Romantic nationalism, effectuated and distributed through literature. Literature has always been considered the nation-building art *par excellence*, whereas visual art has only been accorded such status since 1900. The literary historian Janko Kos put it succinctly as late as 1996: "As in all former periods (before World War II), the main art through which Slovene spiritual history could spell out the truth about itself was literature, above all poetry (Kos 1996)."[2] At this point it was only a question of higher priority, because he held the visual arts of the twentieth century in high esteem—second only to poetry.

Literature and the visual arts have not been treated as competitors in Slovenian history, yet for a long time it was taken for granted that literature was the only art the Slovenes had. The Modernist exaltation of the visual was inaugurated at the end of the nineteenth century by the question of whether Slovene art existed at all. A response was expected from the Slovene Art Association, which had been founded, as it were, for this purpose. Furthermore, the discovery of Slovene art in 1904 by the Viennese critics was perceived as an important step toward Slovenian self-realization as a nation.[3] The visual arts joined literature to become the liberal arts in truest sense (Brejc 1982).[4] The artist Rihard Jakopič (1869–1943) initially believed that Slovene painting did not exist prior to his generation, although he himself contributed a reconstruction of the artistic tradition in the Slovene territories stretching back to the beginning of the century (Rihard Jakopič, 1910). As Francè Stelè (1886–1972) noted in the introduction to his *Outline of History of Art in Slovene Territories* in 1924, Jakopič insisted that Slovene art before 1800 did not exist (Stelè 1924). Slovene art history proved him wrong by revealing a rich artistic heritage in the Slovene territories from the late twentieth century onward.

The reasons for that belated recognition of the visual were manifold and complex. The central issue in Slovene culture of the nineteenth century was the question of identity. As with most nations—and particularly with small ones—it was based on the language that was the province of men of letters and native linguists. We can identify the adjective *Slovene* in the Protestant literature, but it is impossible to distinguish it from the meaning "Slavic". The brief Napoleonic occupation (1809–1813) and the creation of the Illyrian provinces, which cut Austria off from the sea, proved that political options other than the Austrian Empire were possible for a nation located within the smashed Crown of the Holy Roman Empire. The poet Valentin Vodnik (1758–1819) greeted the French as liberators from an enslavement by Germans. In such ways, Slovenes grew aware of their Slavic identity.

Jernej Kopitar published a grammar book of Slavic language in Carniola, Carinthia, and in southern Styria in 1809 (Kopitar 1809).[5] However, he perceived Slavs as a single nation, with a language composed of a variety of dialects, and accordingly envisioned Slavic culture as the third constituency of the empire. Prešeren engaged in a dispute with Kopitar in favor of a distinct Slovene identity and refused the reinvention of the script proposed under Kopitar's influence by Franc Serafin Metelko and Peter Dajnko in 1824 and 1825. The conflict was resolved in the 1830s, and a decade later Prešeren refuted the Illyric movement that strove to amalgamate the Slovene and Croat people through language to create a stronger nation. His claim to a particularly Slovene cultural identity has never been seriously challenged, although various forms of Pan-Slavism outlived the century. Unification under the Serbian crown after the World War I made the national trinity (Serbian–Croat–Slovene) a political requirement. Janko Kos extended this threat to identity to communist rule because the nation was then supposed to melt back into the international proletaria through "brotherhood and unity" (Kos 1996, p. 18).

The enlightened, centralized absolutist state implemented the first program of general education to increase literacy, improve on the agrarian economy, and expand the pool for recruitment into the imperial administration apparatus. The introduction of the first public school system (by imperial decree in 1774) enjoining the use of the local language mapped the national territory and created the audience for and the followers of Romantic nationalist ideas. The actual mass movement could start only after the abolition of land bondage in 1848 and the improvement of the transportation infrastructure. The political leaders were the literati. Only at the time of the so-called camps between 1868 and 1871— political gatherings that brought together tens of thousands of participants—was the political mission gradually transferred onto professional politicians. The moral authority remained with writers such as Fran Levstik (1831–1887) and Josip Stritar (1836–1923).

Figure 1: Peter Pavel Brang, *The German house in Celje* (1905–1906).
(National Gallery of Slovenia)

The difficulty of identification was aggravated by the notion of the purity and unity of the nation. Throughout the century, the idiom "Slovene people" described only the peasant folk: the natural, authentic, good, and morally invincible people patronized by its social and cultural elites, united in common resistance to the foreign (German) assimilation. Fran Levstik still insisted on this vision of the people. Because language had become the principal criterion of identification, anything else was strange (and, under the threat of Germanization, even hostile), making it impossible to integrate cultural diversity, current cultural production, and cultural heritage. For instance, the imperial regulation of construction in the nineteenth century spread the work of Vienna-based architects throughout the empire, which unified the look of public edifices. That phenomenon could never constitute a part of the Slovene identity; it remained "the other." When critics and writers referred to Vienna after the successful 1904 Slovene impressionist exhibition at Galerie Miethke, they claimed that the painters were recognized "abroad."

The criterion for distinguishing "the strange from ours" was language. The German communities in towns dominated the region economically. They created their institutions much earlier than Slovenes. By the end of the century, cultural institutions in the Slovene territories counted four community centers with ballrooms and two theaters in Ljubljana, with one of each in the Styrian towns of Celje and Maribor. The Styrian and the Carniolan edifices followed picturesque medievalist German examples as well as modern Secessionist style for German institutions (such as the German House in Celje, or the German theater in Ljubljana with its unusual Art Nouveau recasting of picturesque motifs), whereas Neo-Renaissance and Baroque styles (including the Slovene theater, which is today the opera house; the community center in Ljubljana (Narodni dom); and both community centers in Celje and Maribor) were pitched against German romanticized picturesque medievalism to demarcate the Slovene institutions. (Fig. 1) As a rule, Czech architects were chosen to design buildings for Slovene investors. A local, exclusive appropriation of the two styles signified the Slovene and the German— or "ours" and "the strange," respectively—in the construction of public institutions and even private villas.[6]

Similarly, the Impressionists were described as "strangers" in attacks on their role in the Art Association exhibition in 1902. They "estranged themselves from the nation," and their art was "strange to our culture" (Malovrh 1902). The whole of Slovene history was understood as people ruled and exploited by "strangers"—that is, Germans. There were tendencies toward particularly "Slovene" forms in Art Nouveau, but they were mainly limited to ornament and decoration. The most daring and somewhat belated proposals came from Ivan Vurnik during the early 1920s, but Janez Jager had worked in this direction in interior decoration before the turn of the century (Zgonik 2002, pp. 35–46). Needless to say, such forms had to be invented, and the exceptional presence of the style of the Secession—or Art Nouveau—in the 1920s can be attributed to the delay caused by the first, albeit ambiguous, national emancipation after the World War I.

Literature also had a greater appeal among the people. National interpellation was met by subscriptions to book series and magazines (Žižek 1987, 1980). Reading was promoted, and it became fashionable to attend social occasions where popular plays were performed, and there was poetry and music. The places or halls where recitals took place were called "reading rooms" [*čitalnice*], and the term for the events was adopted from the Czech language: they were called *béseda*, a word associated with "the word" in Slovene.

Slovene was introduced as the official language in elementary schools in 1873, whereas in secondary schools that happened only after 1908, when demands for a national university were already a habitual topic in the imperial parliament.[7] The visual was limited to the theater and to the national costume, which was obligatory at reading-room functions and parades. National costume meant peasant costume—the fashion of the people—although it was actually a modified version of wealthy peasant attire of the early nineteenth century, itself modeled on Baroque fashions and varied according to provincial tastes.

Socioeconomic reasons were equally important in accounting for the complications and ambiguities of identification, and consequently for the domination of literature. Slovenes were agrarian people throughout their history.[8] The Middle Ages knew the agrarian middle class, called *kosezi*, a libertine peasant population that played an important role in the investiture of dukes, which was performed for the last time in Carinthia in 1414 in the Slovene language. The libertine class disappeared in the fifteenth century, having been integrated either into the lower ranks of the gentry or the enslaved. The towns were small and statistically insignificant in relation to "the people," and the population of towns played no major political role because it was ethnically divided. Abolition of bondage by imperial decree in 1848 opened up the possibility of expansion and the eventual turn of the town population ratio in favor of Slovenes.

The growth of the urban population was further slowed by the economic deprivation of the region. During the nineteenth century, the bourgeoisie were excluded from the constituents of the nation for two reasons: ethnic differences and ethical suspicions. The town was considered to be a place of exploitation and moral corruption. As such, it was strange to the Slovene Catholic identity. The Church thus played perhaps the most significant role in Slovene culture and did not hesitate to engage in political life. Its close surveillance effected a sort of censorship, aimed at protecting the people's moral composure from the seductive provocation of modernization.[9] On the same grounds, the Church reacted against the heralds of modern art.

The middle class structured the political organization in the second half of the nineteenth century, but it never succeeded in controlling Slovene politics because of its own internal divisions. It was divided into the Slovene People's Party, which was impregnated by clericalism and loyalty to the Serbian crown, and the National Progressive Party, which was liberal, Pan-Slavic, and above all—anticlerical. Their constituencies were relatively balanced, so they had to compromise with the German constituency for political advantage. That situation complicated their relation to the people when the political rostrum declared itself as the people's elite. Confrontations between the two parties were seldom productive, because instead of forging and internalizing a vision of the stratified and diversified nation, they struggled to exert hegemony over the people.

With the rise of competent art criticism and with the introduction of art history as an intellectual discipline, the old perspective on the hierarchy of arts was seriously challenged. Not only did art historical research conducted by the National Gallery (at the University of Ljubljana and the Slovene Art History Society) reconstruct the patrimony, it sought out and identified indigenous forms and decorative systems. The first significant conclusion was that the cultural borders did not coincide with the ethnic ones. In short—culture is shared. Second, the new art historical research defined Slovene ethnic territory as transitional and peripheral—Slovenian culture became a place where the cultures of Italy and the Germanic North met and produced their distinct, as well as hybrid, forms. The distinction of high and low art was understood as a dynamic interaction whereby social elites mediated the influence of European centers, whereas local traditions regulated the adaptation and perpetuation of received forms. This integrative effort revealed the important role of the visual culture that reached its peak in the fifteenth and eighteenth centuries.

For example, as early as the second half of the fourteenth century, a standardized iconographic program of the Church as a whole and the altar vault, known as the Carniolan Presbytery, can be identified (Stelè 1969, pp. 38–49).[10] The first eminent scholar of Slovene Gothic fresco painting, France Stelè, emphasized how the style integrated the architectural frame with the iconographic program, giving special attention to decorative details. Stelè noted the significance of decorative elements in the little isolated narratives that are marginal to the large scenes, such as the Procession of the Magi, and even in the decorative frames used to structure the narrative sequence or to organize the painted ceiling of the nave (Stelè 1969, 52–62). Another distinct regional form was *Holy Sunday* (e. g. Crngrob, fresco, pilgrimage church, ca. 1440-1445) —a representation of the Eucharistic Christ and the work not to be performed on Sunday. Four exceptional compositions of the Holy Sunday have been preserved, and in several other locations the Holy Sunday can be identified either through fragments or archival evidence. The type is also known in the broader region—in Tirol and Friuli, besides central Slovenia.[11] On the basis of the Imago Pietatis, it first extended the Arma Christi by including tools of everyday use, setting them beside the arms that injured Christ. In the mid-fifteenth century, the tools were replaced by the representation of labors. The structure is open, a parataxis: scenes spread in horizontal bands around the full figure of Christ pointing at his wounds. It touches on folklore, and comparative material can be found in the humorous scenes and fables, such as the decoration of beehives, which are peculiar to the folk culture of the Slovene territories even today.

Imaging the nation called for political incentives to stimulate visual production. As a consequence, the Slovene Artists' Association was founded in 1899 with the support of the literati and politicians. The first exhibition a year later was a success; special trains were organized for visitors from Trieste and Celje, and tourists were greeted in Ljubljana by a brass band. At the fiasco of the second exhibition of the association two years later, one of the critics in his final punchline commented on what he could not find there: "We want grand, ideal, elevated, national programmatic Slovene art. Give it to us!"[12] That call was answered in 1903 by the painting titled *Slovenia Paying Tribute to Ljubljana* (oil on canvas, 1903, Assembly room, City Hall, Ljubljana), made for the City Hall of Ljubljana. Ivana Kobilca (1863–1926) labored over the commission, which she had received from the Slavophile mayor of Ljubljana, Ivan Hribar. The healthy, happy, beautiful, exotic, unified nation is shown gathering around the throne, which is occupied by a young, fairylike woman—the allegory of Ljubljana. It is important to notice that there is no religious symbol in sight.

Figure 2: *Slovenia Paying Tribute to Ljubljana* (1903).
(National Gallery of Slovenia)

This masquerade of the national reading-room costumes is the liberal vision of the nation venerating its capital, here identified with the National Progressive Party; it may be a response to an image painted by Ivan Grohar (1867–1911). Grohar's talent, because he lacked education, at first earned him the most prestigious church commissions. The recently invested bishop of Ljubljana, Anton Bonaventura Jeglič, dedicated the Slovene people to The Holy Heart of Jesus in 1899 and commissioned this painting for it celebration (oil on canvas, The Diocesan Palace, Ljubljana). The humble folk here are under the tutorship of the Virgin and Margaret of Alacoque (a family with red, white, and blue shared between the parents, and girls in modern dress), while the left side is held by a beggar, an elderly clergyman (?), a girl, and a woman in national costume. This is not the nation: this is the Slovene people, marked by their Catholic piety, hard labor, and modesty. Notice that the bourgeoisie are excluded from the image, which brings the vision within the ideological horizon of Christian Socialism.

The 1907 exhibition in Trieste was an overt manifestation of Slovene culture in the imperial port, where the population was divided approximately into thirds between indigenous Italian and Slovene constituencies; the German population, and other imperial nationalities. However, the reception in Ljubljana was much more significant than in Trieste. Grohar showed his large painting *The Sower* (1907) for the first time, while it still smelled of turpentine. One of the critics writing for the conservative paper *The Slovene* misread Grohar's Impressionist surface as a foggy morning instead of high noon, which the painting was intended to represent, concluding: "This painting must become one of the most popular paintings of our people. It shows not only a piece of our peasant life, but it also reflects our soul" (Anon 1907). Although the image was conceived as one that would entail a measure of local identity, it drew on the Symbolist tradition and used a modernist but somewhat outdated technique; for those reasons it was ignored or criticized abroad.[13] To Slovene audiences *The Sower* (oil on canvas, 1907, Museum of Modern Art, Ljubljana, on loan to the National Gallery of Slovenia) represented the hard-working, enduring Slovene peasant who had preserved the language during a millennium of German domination, marching bravely into the morning fog, warranting the national future. Therefore, we should understand it as the third principal image— sufficiently generalized and aesthetically elevated—to make the image of the nation acceptable across the political spectrum. Grohar's painting achieved the impossible: it offered a unified image of a socially and spiritually differentiated nation.

This consensus in turn legitimized and domesticated Modernism in Slovene art. Grohar's first major painting, *The Spring* (1903, oil on canvas, National Gallery of Slovenia), figured as the central piece in the exhibition of *Freie Vereinigung der Künstlergruppe Sava: Sloweniche Künstler* in Vienna in 1904. In response, Viennese critics recognized a new national school of the empire in their work. The literary historian and art critic Ivan Prijatelj (1876–1956) saw that same landscape, when it was shown in the 1905 Secession exhibition in Vienna, as distinctly Slovene (Prijatelj 1905). The subjective, intimate,

Figure 3: *Holy Heart of Jesus* (1901).
(National Gallery of Slovenia)

Figure 4: *The Sower* (1907).
(National Gallery of Slovenia)

pantheistic embracement of nature in Grohar's personal hour of need resulted in an affinity to poetry that consequently licensed even the most radical ecstatic visions of Rihard Jakopič.

A difficult task was left to the poets Ivan Cankar (1872–1918) and Oton Župančič (1874–1949). They had to explain why painting, inspired by easily identifiable strange sources, could figure as "our" Slovene art. Their arguments were poetic. They adopted the concept of *die Stimmung* [lyrical mood]—at the time a widely used local Viennese term, defined and introduced by Alois Riegl (1899). They tried to describe a particular feeling that betrayed Slovene artists because as Cankar wrote in 1910: "No matter what or how they paint, they will always remain Slovene artists" (Cankar 1910).

The ability to represent the contemporary existential condition appears first in Jožef Petkovšek's (1863–1898) painting *At Home* (oil on canvas, 1889, National Gallery of Slovenia), painted in 1889 and discovered by Jakopič when he reconstructed Slovene artistic tradition in an exhibition in 1910. A most incisive critic, the poet-turned-

Figure 5: *At Home* (1889).
(National Gallery of Slovenia)

prose-writer Ivan Cankar wrote an interpretation that has not lost its validity: the painting, he said, represented the condition of the Slovene elite—the intelligentsia, estranged from its people by years of education abroad. Jakopič used Petkovšek as the missing link between the Impressionists and the narrow thread of nineteenth-century art in Slovenia. This painting remains the most often quoted and paraphrased image in Slovene art.

Post–World War I Expressionism raised objections to the legitimacy of impressionism and proposed its own "Slovene" art. This Expressionism mined the heritage of the Secession and *fin-de-siècle* Symbolism and reworked it through Futurism and Cubo-Expressionism. The artists met in Prague, where most of them had studied; they claimed to "nationalize" their art through Primitivism and specifically by the application of techniques and styles found in Slovene folk art. The brothers Kralj are prominent examples; they were born into the family of a self-taught sculptor. The Expressionist phase coincided with the consolidation of post-war Europe that brought a raw deal to Slovenes. Tone Kralj (1900–1975) produced his painting *On the Ruins* (oil on canvas, Božidar Jakac Art Museum, Kostanjevica an Krki) in 1921/1922.

Its political subject remained hidden, and the painting was misinterpreted as the ruins of the empire. In fact it represents the ruins of the 1848 Program of the United Slovenia. The Slovene territory was partitioned among Austria (by the Carinthian Plebiscite of 1919), Italy (in the Rapallo Treaty of 1920) and Yugoslavia, so that less than two-thirds of the ethnic territory remained. High expectations of independence turned sour by the partitioning of the Fatherland. The feeling of despair, dismay, and lack of perspective was effectively expressed by the local version of Expressionism. The style was immediately accepted by the public, but it lasted only three to four years before the first symptoms of resignation into the more abstract world of aesthetics occurred. *Neue Sachlichkeit* (New Objectivity) quickly replaced the critical voice of Expressionism.

The visual arts started to gather momentum as their institutions came into existence: the first public exhibition space opened in 1909, professional art criticism appeared, and so did modern patterns of patronage, and the art market. They were followed by the foundation of the National Gallery in 1918, the Art Historical Society with its magazine, the fine arts department at the university, and a fine arts academy in 1945. The Museum of Modern Art was first planned in 1936, and the building was constructed in 1950.

After a brief period of the Socialist Realism, the Yugoslav regime began searching for a separate identity, and the visual arts were once more a powerful means of self-identification. In the Slovene case, the Impressionists were cleansed of their bourgeois stigmata, and their paintings were reconfirmed as national icons. It was only then that Grohar rose to the stature of "the most Slovene" of the Impressionists. In Yugoslavia, the Impressionists were also beneficiaries of the fact that they were the most articulate group that had emerged from the private school of the Slovene painter Anton Ažbe (1862–1905) in Munich, where a considerable number of other Slavic students had studied.

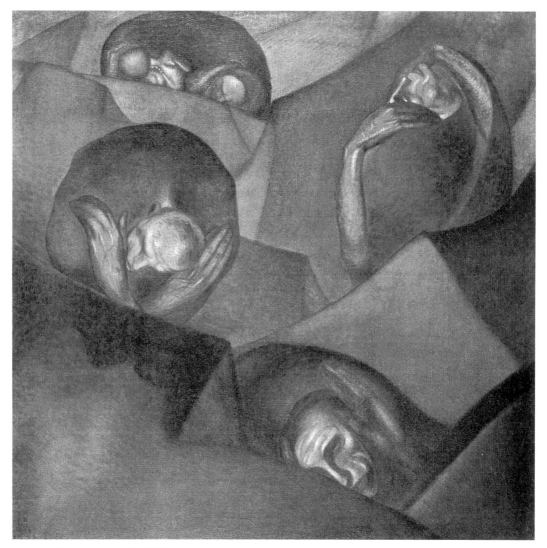

Figure 6: *On the Ruins* (1921/1922)
(Božidar Jakac Art Museum, Kostanjevica na Krki).

Visual culture was strongly supported and subsidized by the government. The Ljubljana School of Printmakers was promoted throughout the (third) world as a representation of Slovene art: Božidar Jakac, France Mihelič, Riko Debenjak, Marjan Pogačnik, and Vladimir Makuc, followed by their students Janez Bernik, Andrej Jemec, Bogdan Borčič, and Adriana Maraž, to name just a few. The International Biennial of Graphic Arts remains the longest-running event in Slovenia. (By the mid-1970s, Slovenia could claim more than two hundred galleries and exhibition spaces but not a

Figure 7: *Terror = Décor* (1997)
(Obalne galerije, Piran, exh. catalog 2000).

single commercial gallery!) The generation of their teachers was still concerned with the authentic and indigenous to produce a new regional identity. The next generation was already in resonance with international developments, and it began eagerly casting away everything that could signify the periphery.

In 1985, the IRWIN group launched the project Slovene Athens, which ended with an exhibition in the Museum of Modern Art in Ljubljana in 1991. They set out to deconstruct the ideology of national identity in visual art, by paraphrasing and ironizing the outstanding images and signs of Slovene national patrimony. IRWIN organized forty-three artists to respond to the specifically Slovene Modernist experience. In IRWIN's own case, a shadow of a sower is cast over many of the symbols and signs that comprise Slovene mental heraldry, including the sea, the mountains, nature, the cave (*Karst*), and the hayrack—all of them shown under the historic images of the Virgin, the protector of the nation (IRWIN, *Slovene Athens: The Sea, Thea karst, The Fields, The Woods, The Alps*, 1987 (340 x 160 cm each!), Ludwigsforum, Aachen, Germany).

The visual imagery of Žiga Kariž is inspired by the media, television in particular. Television brings the world to one's living room. For Kariž, TV fills one's life with images, most of them irrelevant, and we tend not to notice, not to distinguish, not to care, nor understand—basically, we do not want to be bothered. Kariž took a peculiar rhyme as his title: *Terror = Décor* (1997, Obalne galerije, Piran); the rhyme is pregnant with meanings meant to unveil the reality of our existence. He started out in 1998 with enlargements of film stills to produce fuzzy images painted on canvas—they were images turned into a pure surface, obliterating their truth and the reality of their sources. The paintings, framed by an ornamental design (a stickerlike kitchen scene pasted into the composition), turned into decorative and beautiful ornaments in our reality. That perverse obliteration was well described by Andrej Medved: "Reality is beautiful, the truth is dreadful" (Kariž 2000)

Kariž expanded his concept in 2000 by including a surveillance camera and a warning system in the painting: the *Décor* had become an instrument of terror. In *Terror = Décor* (1997), the beautiful object not only returns our gaze but it monitors us watching it. The images on the surface of the *Terror = Décor* (1997) are stills of explosions, but the object itself contains an explosive that can be activated, exploded—the truth brought back to reality, so to speak. Suddenly, an alarm goes off and a light flashes, informing the owner he is only seconds away from an explosion: he needs to leave his apartment immediately. The owner of the *Terror = Décor* (1997) listens to the ticking of the bomb within the painting within the walls of his apartment. Under the surface of our high-tech reality, a bomb is ticking—the bomb of conflict in global economic exploitation (Kariž 2003).[14]

An examination of nineteenth- and twentieth-century cultural history thus reveals a few facts about the relationship of the visual and the literary that are not self-evident. National emancipation and the formation of the nation, concluded at the end of the century, depended largely on language and were conducted by men of letters. Paradoxically, they were assisted by state institutions, which implemented literary education. National emancipation created the false impression that Slovenes were oriented predominantly toward literarity. Complex social, economic, and psychological circumstances extended the process of national identification and social differentiation as preconditions to nationhood. As that process drew to a close, it was painting that could synthesize images of the Slovene existential condition, as in Petkovšek; of the Slovene nation, embodied in Grohar's image of *The Sower* (1907); and of political reality, as evidenced in Expressionist imagery and in Tone Kralj's *On the Ruins* (1921/1922) in particular. That triumph of the visual was matched by art historical research that redefined the share of art in Slovene cultural history from the late twelfth century onward. Starting with Stelè's *Outline of the History of Art with Slovenes* in 1924, an interaction of the center and periphery, producing a regionally authentic heritage, replaced the earlier model of artistic importation, retardation, and inadequacy to the standards of the center.

In the twentieth century, uncertainties fed the need to reexamine, redefine, rework, and improve sensitivity to tradition and to produce a new and authentic Slovene art. France Kralj was a tragic victim of that effort; he insisted, ultimately without effect, on authentic Slovene art from the 1930s to his early death in 1960. The Intimists of the 1950s still busied themselves with the question of what might comprise typical and authentic Slovene art. One product of those initiatives is the parties at the table whose outstanding representation is found in Pregelj's *The Table of Pompeii* (oil on canvas, 1962, ‚Museum of Modern Art, Ljubljana). IRWIN's ironic twist swept away the ambiguities of identity by deconstructing the national ideologies of the past. That was the first step toward the self-confidence with which Žiga Kariž could raise issues of universal interest in Ljubljana, Venice, New York, or any cultural capital of the world.

References

Rihard Jakopič (1910), *80 let upodabljajoče umetnosti na Slovenskem*, Ljubljana: Jakopičev paviljon.

Anon (1902), "Druga slovenska umetniška razstava," *Slovenec*, 30 (222, September 27), pp 1–2.

Anon (1907), " Prva slovesnka umetniška razstava v Trstu," *Slovenec*, 35 (246, October 24) pp. 1–2.

Brejc, Tomaž (1982), *Slovenski impresionisti in evropsko slikarstvo*, Ljubljana: Partizanska knjiga.

Cankar, Ivan (1899), *Erotika*, Ljubljana: Kleinmayr & Bamberg.

Cankar, Ivan (1910), "Naši umetniki II," *Slovenski narod*, 43 (67, March 24), p. 1.

Kariž, Žiga (2000), *Teror = dekor*, Galerija Loža, Koper, Slovenija.

Kariž, Žiga (2003), *ART NOW, Žiga Kariž*, 50th Venice Biennial, Slovene Pavillion, Venice, Italy.

Kopitar, Jernej (1809), *Gramatik der Slawishen Sprache in Krain, Kärnten und Steiermark*Laibach: Wilhelm Heinrich Korn.

Kos, Janko (1996), *Duhovna zgodovina Slovencev*, Ljubljana: Slovenska matica.

Malovrh, Miroslav (1902), "'Tujci.' II. Slovenska umetniška razstava," *Novice*, 60 (no. 40), p. 392.

Mikuž, Jure (1985) "Les Impressionistes slovènes: Une expression politique en 1904," *Revue d'esthethique,* NS no. 9, 169–174.

National and University Library (2004), *Rojstni list slovenske culture,* Ljubljana, 17 May–20 June. Ljubljana: National and University Library.

Prijatelj, Ivan (1905), " Dunajska secesija III," *Slovenski narod,* 38 (76, April 3), p. 1.

Riegl, Alois (1899), "Die Stimmung als Inhalt der modernen Kunst," *Graphiche Künste, XXII,* Vienna, pp. 47–56.

Stelè, Francè (1924), *Oris zgodovine umetnosti pri Slovencih: Kulturnozgodvinski poskus.* Ljubljana, ? Nova založba .

Stelè, Francè (1969), *Slikarstvo v Sloveniji od 12. do 16.* stoletja, Ljubljana: Slovenska matica.

Zgonik, Nadja (2002), *Podobe Slovenstva,* Ljubljana: Nova revija.

Žižek, Slavoj, "Ideologija in estetski učinek." In ?name of editor(s)?, (1980), *Louis Althusser: Ideologija in ideološki aparati države.* Ljubljana: Cankarjeva založba.

Žižek, Slavoj (1986), *Jezik, ideologija, Slovenci,* Ljublajna: Delavska enotnost.

Endnotes

1. Fran Miklošič (1813–1891), later in 1848 the key figure at drafting of the United Slovenia program, recommended omitting certain verses to Prešeren to avoid political complications. In 1844, the poem did not pass censorship and was published only after abolition of censorship in *Novice (The News)* on 26 April 1848, in the wake of the March Revolution.

2. "Kot v vseh prejšnjih obdobjih je poglavitna umetnost, skozi katero je slovenska duhovna zgodovina lahko izrekla resnico o sebi, ostajala literatura, predvsem poezija."

3. Ivan Cankar had already written about historic achievements of Slovene culture in his response to the 1904 exhibition; that achievement, in a nutshell, was the mode of the Slovene painter's address of the Viennese audiences in a familiar and current visual language—neo-impressionism, symbolism, Monetschule, and others.

4. Recent art historical literature refers to that development as the nobilitation of arts in Slovene culture—for example, Tomaž Brejc, Jure Mikuž (1985), and others.

5. Jernej Kopitar (1780–1844), the leading scholar on Slavic languages and literatures, scriptor at the Imperial Library and Imperial censor appointed by Prince Clemens Wenzel Lothar von Metternich (1773–1859), was a controversial and ideologically stigmatized figure. He identified the origin of the Freising manuscripts and critically evaluated the Protestant literature, yet censoring of Prešeren's poetry was a sin that seemed irredeemable to every schoolgirl or schoolboy since the introduction of the Slovene language in educational institutions in 1874. The reproduction of the doublecrossed *The Toast* was published in secondary school textbooks and it was added in facsimile of the Prešeren's book of poetry in 1966.

6. One of the most beautiful villas belonged to the painter Heinrich Wettach, a member and a soloist at the German-dominated Philharmonic Society. Wettach immigrated to Austria in 1918. In 1902 even a more declaratively modern, Secessionist style was described as "strange, imported" and thus degenerate—strange—to the Nation.

7. Demonstrations that year provoked gunfire from the policing forces, leaving two men dead—Lunder and Adamič, whose name has been assigned to the most prominent quai, newly redeveloped under the earthquake reconstruction.

8. Note the similarities and distinctions in Kris van Heuckleom's discussion of Poland, in this volume.

9. The bishop of Ljubljana Anton Bovantura Jeglič bought all the available copies of Ivan Cankar's first book of poetry entitled *Erotika* (1899) and burnt them.

10. The northern wall of the nave, usually without windows, was reserved for the procession of the Magi and the Epiphany; the arched wall of the presbytery was set aside for Cain and Abel's sacrifice and the Annunciation or else St. George and the Dragon; and the southern wall was given to the legend of the patron saint. The exterior of the church continued the imaging of the world. The obligatory St. Christopher was always on the wall facing the village. Votive images, saints, representations of Golgotha, sometimes The Last Judgement, and perhaps the Imago Pietatis appeared without any fixed location or relation to other images (see Stelè 1969).

11. A similar motif existed in Britain, where it was known as Pier's Plowman (Stelè 1969, 27–32).

12. "Mi pa si želimo velike, idealne, vzvišene, narodne, programne umetnosti slovenske. Dajte nam jo!" (Druga slovenska umetniška razstava 1902).

13. The critical response in Krakow and Warsaw in 1908 was negative.

14. See Kariz (2003). The publication includes the third stage of the project, expanding the aesthetic object into interactive installations and simultaneous production.

Lost In Translation, or *Nothing* to See But Everything

Sunil Manghani

> The text does not "gloss" the images, which do not "illustrate" the text. For me, each has been no more than the onset of a kind of visual uncertainty, analogous perhaps to that *loss of meaning* Zen calls a *satori*. Text and image, interlacing, seek to ensure the circulation and exchange of these signifiers: body, face, writing; and in them to read the retreat of signs
>
> – Roland Barthes, *Empire of Signs*

In this paper I want to draw critical purpose from a recurring trope (from a "Western" perspective) of "being lost" in Japan. I wrote most of this account while staying at my parent-in-law's house in Tokyo. I am not Japanese myself, nor do I speak the language (at least not yet!). And, in truth, it is only recently that I have gained any real experience of Japanese culture. Nonetheless, I intend to make some virtue out of my

A study space to fold and put away—everyday a new place from which to write… (Photo: Author).

circumstance. Indeed, I write intentionally as a visitor to a culture, as a visitor to Japan, to show how I think it makes for a visual curiosity that is pertinent to understanding and engaging in a visual literacy. I am not going to draw from my own adventures in Japan as such but instead look at the trope of being lost—one that is evident in a brief selection of cultural incidents, both verbal and visual. My key text is Roland Barthes's often overlooked *Empire of Signs* (1983). It is fair to say I am not entirely convinced there is any definable thing we might call "visual literacy" about which can be discussed or written. Instead, it is something you need best orient yourself in, or *visit*.

The open architecture of this visual literacy might suitably be thought comparable to the conditions under which I wrote much of this article, sitting, as I did, on the floor of a traditional Japanese room (a room of six *tatami* mats and sliding *shoji* panels at the windows). Each morning, before I could began to work, I first had to put away the futon and find places to hide my ever-growing pile of clothes and other belongings. I would then slide the window panels into what I felt was the optimum configuration for a comfortable working light. Finally, I would clear the way to set up my workspace: laptop on a low chair or table, and books and things strewn about my folded legs (which soon would be aching). Every day offered a new unrepeatable place from which to write, perhaps not unlike the "moment" Barthes describes when one takes a photograph, "very carefully (in the Japanese manner) but having neglected to load the camera with film" (Barthes 1983, p. 83). The point of which is not to lament such circumstance but to turn any potential disappointment or sense of the unattainable into a critical reflection. More generally, I think this is what visiting Japan might appear for many to offer. Perhaps it has *nothing* to do with Japan as such, though everything to do with having been there—having had its spaces in which to think. As Jonathan Crary reminds us, with great acuity: "We've been trained to assume that an observer will always leave visible tracks, that is, will be identifiable in terms of images." But, as with the observer Crary documents, here too, "it's a question of an observer who takes shape in other, grayer practices and discourses" ([Crary] 1988, p. 43). I can only really offer a few brief snapshots, though hopefully these can prove enough in getting at what I want to say. Besides, this paper is hardly concerned with an enquiry into Japan, imposing an interpretation, or applying a semiotics, but rather letting, as Barthes does, its destination unwind to reveal the situation as it *is*—not to locate or center meaning but instead to ride its very transport.

1

One-way Street: A (Western) visitor to Japan—certainly one who does not speak (or, more specifically read) the language—is likely to experience a sense of confusion and dislocation upon arrival. Of course, this is the case for a visitor anywhere in the world. Yet, somehow, Japan (or, perhaps more accurately Tokyo) seems a peculiarly alluring place for those

Ginza, Toyko (2003)
(Photo: Author).

intending to get lost. It is a "myth today" foretold by a whole raft of literatures, films, and ephemera, each exoticizing the pleasures of its dislocation and culture. And the fantasy is not always about a pleasure in getting lost. In his account of a visit to Tokyo with his 12-year-old son, Peter Carey is a little perturbed to find it is not quite what he had *imagined*, especially when his fanciful misunderstandings of the culture are neatly solved, leaving just mundane certainty (Carey 2005). And echoing Alex Kerr's lament for a purported decline in the traditional culture of Japan (Kerr, 1996), Carey is only really able to find *his* "Japan" in a theater full of tourists, during a four-hour Kabuki performance (and even that does not fully absorb him). The situation is even worse for Carey's son, whose manga-filled fantasies are most certainly more adequately catered for by visiting his local comic shop in New York than by being dragged around places of historic and cultural interest in the real Japan! Being lost in Japan is not only about being lost in the country of Japan but rather in a certain aesthetic experience we attribute to it.

Significantly, the enigma of "being lost" would seem a particularly visual one, with all engagement (as Barthes is want to suggest) based upon witnessing and gesturing, than straight-forward conversing. Yet, how is it one culture can be more visual than another? In Tokyo, the topos of its visual allure would seem to arise mostly from what Paul Waley suggests is its "lack of visual order." This, he argues, "both stimulates and enrages the foreign observer," for how, he asks, can "a city be both clean and cluttered? How can it be both immensely drab and provocatively colourful?" (Waley 1992). It is, seemingly, a need to temper this chaos that draws in the viewer/visitor—clearly for Waley it provides the excuse for his numerous didactic articles published in the *Japan Times*. Barrie Shelton's *Learning from the Japanese City* (1999) is an obvious example of an engagement with such edifying visual intrigue. Following his initial bafflement, irritation, and even intimation on visiting the Japanese city, Shelton retrieves inspiration and vitality from what he sees, using it to rethink the cityspace of the West—hence, as the title implies, his book presents a kind of Japanese-related version of "learning from Las Vegas" (Venturi et al., 1977).

Of course, the disorderly perception is due in large part to an ignorance of the characters in Japanese writing, which prompts a complete collapse in any readable sign system. It is not simply that the language is unknown to the visitors, but that this lack of knowledge is made visible everywhere you go: "Neon, billboards, street signs, posters, liquid-crystal displays, they are all signs containing signs, the written signs of the Japanese language. It is a notable irony that there should be so much to read in the streets of a city so hard to decipher" (Waley 1992, p. 15). It is a myth associated with this visual array that Barthes's *Empire of Signs* (1983) both embraces and builds out of for critical purpose. Significantly, for Barthes, it is a distinctly happy (even utopian) myth or fantasy, finally giving respite from that "science" of semiotics he did so much to establish. For in his *fictional* Japan he can seek: "The dream: to know a foreign (alien) language and yet not to understand it: to perceive the difference in it without that difference ever being recuperated by the superficiality of discourse, communication or vulgarity." For Barthes this is not so much to comment upon Japan and its culture (although he does do this) but rather "to undo [his] own 'reality' under the effect of other formulations, other syntaxes …in a word, to descend into the untranslatable, to experience its shock without ever muffling it" (Barthes 1983, p. 6).

In allowing himself to be lost in or without translation, Barthes seeks to assert or designate a particular freedom from the West's purported obsession with meaning. Indeed, the Japanese culture/screen—as with its distinctive sliding *shoji* panels—supposedly provides a visual experience, a hall of mirrors for the West to hold up to itself. The mirror is not, as Barthes points out, a narcissistic object but rather a mirror that empties out: "it is the symbol of the very emptiness of symbols ('*The mind of the perfect man*,' says one Tao master, '*is like a mirror. It grasps nothing but repulses nothing. It receives but does not retain*'): the mirror intercepts only other mirrors, and this infinite reflection is emptiness itself" (Barthes 1983, p. 79). In his empire of empty, open signs—

with attention upon the run or travel of signs, rather than their fixity—Barthes is not attempting to secure any "enormous labour of *knowledge*," to learn and codify all of the Orient.[1] His indulgence in the recurring trope of Japan's dizzying panorama is to search out "not other symbols but the very fissure of the symbolic" (Barthes 1983, p. 4). In this way, Barthes attempts to situate (without finally locating) his inclination for a "new semiology"—one in which the semiologist is more "an artist" playing with signs "as with a conscious decoy, whose fascination he savours and wants to make others savour and understand." As he puts it, this kind of semiology is "not a hermeneutics: it paints more than it digs" (Barthes 2000, p. 475).

In part, Barthes's *Empire of Signs* (1983) can be thought of as a deconstructive fiction, for it is a kind of antidote, or "supplement" to the myth of Japan that it constructs. Yet, equally scattered throughout the text are bits and pieces that refuse to be deconstructed, a symptom of which is that there is no complexity to be found, there is not the kind of elaboration or elongation (as in duration, or *différance*) that might usually be associated with deconstruction. Instead, withdrawing from "analysis," Barthes rather takes the haiku as his emblem, noting for us that "the brevity of the haiku is not formal; the haiku is not a rich thought reduced to a brief form, but a brief event which immediately finds its proper form" (Barthes 1983, p. 75). Thus, quite apart from all the "talk" (or "talking over") of a deconstruction as a means to achieving dialogue with the subaltern (see Spivak 1988), in *Empire of Signs* (1983), Barthes attempts to give us situations of writing as "spaces" (or, even pauses) in which another voice might be heard. Situations, then, in which "we" are photographed, not the other way round (. . . or, *as if we are spotted wandering the wrong way up a one-way street!*). And so, we encounter another writing entirely—a visual writing perhaps, or at least a writing *with* images (and not about them).

2

Sandcastles: It has always surprised me that *Empire of Signs* (Barthes 1983) has received such little critical attention. This is especially strange within the context of visual culture studies (a "field" frequently hailing Barthes as one of its founding figures), because in this book Barthes not only writes but also *pictures* his thoughts. One specific reservation is most likely a perceived political incorrectness, making this perhaps the politely forgotten text of our otherwise unblemished master of mythologies. Yet, for me, it is precisely *because* of its indulgence in another culture that I have wanted to bring it to attention. I take a similar line here to Martin Jay when, in opposing the "triumph of cultural relativism in visual terms," he argues we accept something of the "excess" of the image; an excess preventing figurality from being entirely reduced to discursivity. Much of the power of images, he suggests, "comes precisely from their ability to resist being entirely subsumed under the protocols of specific cultures." As an example, he reminds us of the silent film, "which

See for yourself, turn it upside down, you can look all you like…
(Photograph of Shikidai Gallery adapted from Barthes' *Empire of Signs* [1983]).

swiftly transcended the boundaries of the specific culture out of which it emerged to achieve global success" (Jay 2002, pp. 271, 275, 274).[2] Perhaps a more deep-rooted reason for the obscurity of Barthes's slim volume on Japan is that there has never been found a use for the excess of its imagery. If we accept James Elkins's pondering over *Camera Lucida* (Barthes 1981) as giving an irrevocable critique of visual studies, then *Empire of Signs* (Barthes 1983) might be thought to actually take us *into* that critique (Elkins 2003, p. 193). It is the puzzle (or, to use Barthes's favored word, *adventure*) we must toy with in pursuing visual studies. Its problematic can be illustrated immediately and very plainly. For, unlike the ruse of the hidden photograph of Barthes's mother, photographed as a child, "found" in *Camera Lucida* (Barthes 1981), the *Empire of Signs* (Barthes 1983) affords us something much more obvious but potentially more profound. At the very "heart" of the book (replicating what Barthes suggests is Tokyo's empty, forbidden, and indifferent center around which the entire city turns) is a photograph of the Shikidai gallery at Nido Castle, Kyoto. Underneath this he writes only: "Turn the image upside down: nothing more, nothing else, nothing" (Barthes 1983, pp.30–32, 50–51).

In this gallery space (which, like "the ideal Japanese house" is bare of any furniture) Barthes finds what he has been looking for all along because the center is rejected ("painful frustration for Western man, everywhere 'furnished' with his armchair, his bed, proprietor of a domestic *location*"). This decentered space becomes fully reversible: "you can turn the Shikidai gallery upside down and nothing would happen," Barthes tells us, "the content is irretrievably dismissed: whether we pass by, cross it, or sit down on the floor (or the ceiling, if you reverse the image), there is nothing to *grasp*" (Barthes 1983, p. 109). If this is the lesson Barthes learns from his time in Japan, we too are given nothing to grasp but the very "onset of a kind of a visual uncertainty" (as Barthes puts it in his opening "methodological" statement)—or as I am framing it here, a kind of visual literacy. The "uncertainty" of this "nothing" is not intended as means to a de-disciplinary or de-skilling exercise as such. Instead, it is meant in a positive, revealing sense—it does not erase or frame but rather opens out to new possibilities. This nothingness to which Barthes refers is inflected by the Buddhist meaning of *mu* [emptiness] or the Zen *satori* [occurrence, or realization]. Western translation, he points out, is only vaguely met by Christian words such as illumination, revelation, and intuition—none of which grasp the sense of breach or exemption from meaning while still implying critical engagement meant by the former "oriental" terms. If anything, translation here only loads meaning upon them (Barthes 1983, p. 75).

Thus, in being a visitor to Japan—a partaker in its ways—Barthes finds "a special organisation of space" allowing him a new situation of writing, an untapped opportunity to think *with* and not only *of* things. He is afforded the time for a more modest kind of travelling: "I am never besieged by the horizon (and its whiff of dreams)," he tells us, "I am limitless without the notion of grandeur, without a metaphysical reference" (Barthes 1983, p. 107). Here, then, is offered an unconditional freedom, delivering him from the heavy metaphysics of Western thought and culture that he frequently castigated. *Empire of Signs* (Barthes 1983) is the light to the dark room of *Camera Lucida*.[3] And unlike the "photographic *ecstasy*" he arrives at there, "obliging the loving and the terrified consciousness to return to the very letter of Time" (Barthes 1982, p. 119), in Japan "the empire of signifiers is so immense, so in excess of speech, that the exchange of signs remains of a fascinating richness, mobility, and subtlety" (Barthes 1983, p. 9) Here, his realization of "intractable reality" is not hostage to the death-mask of "that which has been" but to something much less burdensome. Instead, we are brought "out," alive, into the lightness of his ideas or "theory." For, like the haiku form he turns our attention to, what Barthes suggests we witness is everything, yet *nothing* [*mu*]; indeed only "pure and sole designation. *It's that, it's thus*, says the haiku, *it's so*. Or better still: *so!*" (Barthes 1983, p. 83).

3

Depth-Charge: The outsider's sense of disorder and delight in the surfaces of Japanese culture affords the possibility of seeing images *as* images—no translation required. All too often it is as if we think images must always be full of meaning, when in fact they may be just *there*, ready (though not necessarily willing) to take on these meanings we attribute to them, although—as W. J. T. Mitchell ruefully points out (Mitchell 1996)—we never really stop to ask about that possibility. Instead, we more readily choose to pose all sorts of puzzles about images, as if somewhere within them there is an answer of sorts— the images' *full* meaning. As if, were we to look hard enough (like children poring over picture puzzles to spot the difference or uncover a hidden surprise), we might eventually find "it" recessed in among the more obvious, immediate impression of the picture.

With the advent of digital visual technologies, this image "interior," as I will call it, would seem to have come ever more to the surface of everyday life. To illustrate the point, let me recall that well-known scene in Ridley Scott's *Blade Runner* (Scott 1982) in which Rick Deckard "loads" a photograph into his "Esper machine," asking it ("Pan right and pull back. Stop" and so on) to scan its surface as he searches for a "clue." The distinctive feature of this machine is its ability for image *enhancement*, to convert from low-grade to high-grade resolution; in fact, this means sharpening the focus of something that previously had not really (or rather, digitally) existed. The fanciful technology of the Esper machine represents an imaging apparatus or desire prevalent in popular consciousness, reappearing in various guises in countless high-tech film and television productions. Its function (usually at pivotal moments in the diegesis) is always to mine the depths of an image to reveal a hidden meaning—a vital clue enhanced many times from seemingly nowhere. All of which is of course complete fallacy. As anyone will know from clicking repeatedly on the ubiquitous "zoom" icon in an image program, as you move deeper into a computer-generated picture all you really get to see are increasingly abstract images of color block formations. In fact, with each click of the button, you are generating whole new images, sometimes of quite wondrous proportions. The bottom line, however, is a pixel landscape divided up by a uniform grid.

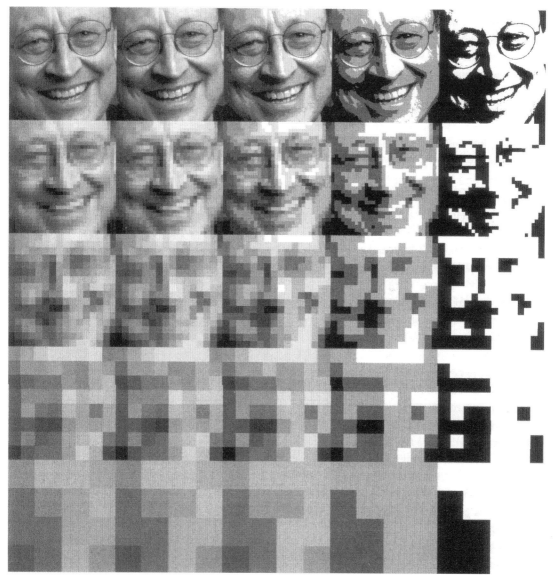

Illustration from William J. Mitchell's *The Reconfigured Eye* (1994) showing varying effects of pixelation. (Courtesy of William J. Mitchell).

As William J. Mitchell demonstrates, when taken in isolation, a single pixel "depicts nothing in particular — merely 'light thing' or 'dark thing'" (Mitchell 1994, p. 67). It is as if here we locate what Mieke Bal refers to as the subsemiotic. These "elements," she argues, are the technical aspects of any given image that, while contributing to the construction of signs, "are not, a priori, signs in themselves; not any more than in a literary text sheer ink on the page, mere punctuation marks, and syntactic structures are" (Bal 1991, p. 400). Yet, as Bal argues, these seemingly superfluous details are what allow an initial "passive gaze" to convert into the dynamic "activity of the viewer," whereby the "work no longer stands alone … [rather] the viewer must acknowledge that he or she make it work" (Bal 1991, p. 4). It is an argument that James Elkins contests, finding that the picture *as picture* is swept away by Bal's analysis into a narrative that is essentially separate from it (in other words, we travel *away* from the picture to *say* something about it; see Elkins 1995, 1996; Bal 1996; Manghani, 2003). By contrast, Elkins is interested in "trying not to practice the kinds of interpretation that explain marks by revealing them as signs." Instead, it is a "wonder" experienced "before the discovery" of details that he wishes to preserve (Elkins 1996, p. 591). Of course, this can seem both all too easy and difficult at the same time. Too easy in that it requires no (conceptual) tools or artifice, too difficult in that it is not simply an all-engulfing, quixotic vision we wish to behold but one nonetheless still requiring our critical engagement.[4] It is undoubtedly this same fine line that I want to suggest is risked when visiting "Japan," for here, all such wonder—before the discovery of details, or rather before the need of a translation—is lost as to be found.

4

百聞一見にしかず[5]: At this juncture—though hardly rivalling Barthes's invitation to turn everything upside down—I can perhaps pose my own "turning point." In this case, a "brief encounter" taken from Sofia Coppola's acclaimed film *Lost in Translation* (Coppola 2003). Again, this film presents us with a version of finding oneself by being lost in Japan, the story being of two Americans "lost" in Tokyo.[6] They are not so much dislocated in geographical or cultural terms (indeed, for the most part they stay within the confines of a high-class international hotel, barely experiencing the "local" culture), instead they are more emotionally and spiritually lost. Bob is an aging, has-been movie star in town to shoot a whiskey commercial, while Charlotte is a young wife tagging along with her somewhat inane, workaholic husband. Lonely and wracked by jetlag-induced insomnia, the two come to know each other in the all-night bar of the hotel. Subsequently, they develop an intimate (platonic) understanding of one another and together find themselves venturing outside, acquainting themselves with the city and its people. As the film blurb puts it, "they ultimately discover a new belief in life's possibilities." Yet, in the end we are to know little of these possibilities, for as the film draws to a close, we the spectators must draw back. Having once already gone their separate ways (parting with something of an unfulfilled goodbye), Bob happens to see Charlotte from the window of his taxi as she melds with a passing crowd. He runs out after her, she turns around and they come together one last time. In an embrace that is as if to kiss, the two whisper into each other's ears; we, however, can only grasp the faint respiration of their words, leaving us with what Barthes would surely describe as a "murmuring mass of an unknown language," and thereby taking us into an interstice, "delivered from any fulfilled meaning" (Barthes 1983, p. 9).

What is unusual and even refreshing about this film is that there is no real development, no deepening plot. Instead, this is a film of episodes or tableaux, each suggestive and slow, accumulating to the point at which we think we might indeed be given an ending, only to find it dissipate. Like the elaborate wrapping of Japanese gifts that so fascinated Barthes (wherein it is as if "the box were the object of the gift, not what it contains"), this film is all about an unwrapping and not what is then found at the end, at its "core" (Barthes 1983, p. 46). Of course, this is not to suggest the close of the film is *devoid* of meaning, for, again like the gift wrapping Barthes observes, this "package is not empty, but emptied" (Barthes 1983, p. 46). It hardly matters how many times you watch this film—you will never need to know what they say to each other, you will only need to witness them saying it. To appropriate a Japanese saying, it would seem a perfect case in which, with the sound permanently on low, "a hundred hearings will never equal the one viewing"; a viewing that in *itself*—like the pixels of a digital image—has no further depth to it, no riddle to be solved. For again, like the haiku, this confidential (though hardly concealed) encounter is "not a rich thought reduced to a brief form, but a brief event which immediately finds its proper form" (Barthes 1983, p. 75).

5

Roundabout: Without wishing to conclude this paper as such—to reduce an array of possibilities and thoughts to a brief summary—I can perhaps allow it to find its proper form by closing with one last illustration: in this case, Sengai Gibon's (1750–1837) rather well-known Zen-inspired artwork *Circle, Triangle, and Square*. This ink painting, on first viewing at least, may seem lacking in any great complexity. On closer inspection it is apparent that rather than a single consistency of black or gray, the ink tones fluctuate continuously, a difficult technical achievement in this medium. Yet, still, its very simplicity is what makes it all the more curious. The simple geometric forms overlap each other, suggesting interconnection, but with no clear meaning. Zen masters—as a part of meditative, controlled thought—would often paint just a circle, and from their writings it is known the meaning of this singular form can relate to all manner of things, including the universe, the void, the moon, and even a rice cake! Yet Gibon paints a triangle and a square too. Many interpretations have been suggested for this: the forms of the mandala and the pagoda; the earth, humanity, and heaven; the Buddha, Buddhist laws, and the Buddhist community; three forms of Buddhism; three schools of Zen, and

Sengai Gibon (1750-1837) *Circle, Triangle, and Square*
(Courtesy of Idemitsu Museum of Arts, Tokyo).

so forth. Yet, such explanations seem of little benefit. As Stephen Addiss remarks, "[t]he actual experience of Sengai's art is what counts, and commentaries are useful only when they take us toward the painting, not away into abstract concepts" (Addiss, 1996, p. 66).

I particularly like this travelling idea of being taken *toward* something—though not as to disturb something but to be in the same (mental) place. And, pertinent to debates in visual literacy, Addiss goes on to remind us: "In Zen, as in art, words are secondary; seeing is primary. Perhaps Sengai's painting means just what it is: a circle, a triangle, and a square" (Addiss 1996 p. 66). Indeed, when—in all curiosity—we come to consider this ink painting (to think about it, or to view it, but without disturbing it!), we might then *see*—*So!*—all of its meaning might indeed be lost in translation, might become superfluous. The only thing we really need "know" is what is here before us: *nothing*, but everything that the shapes allow. It is a particular moment of un-knowledge, or visual literacy, that most likely is not best thought of "at home" on the pages of an essay such as this but instead to be found written elsewhere in dialogues with faraway places we can but visit . . .

References

Addiss, Stephen (1996), *How to Look at Japanese Art*, New York: Harry N. Abrams.

Bal, Mieke (1991), *Reading Rembrandt: Beyond the Word-Image Opposition*, Cambridge: Cambridge University Press.

Bal, Mieke (1996), "Semiotic Elements in Academic Practices," *Critical Inquiry*, 22 (3), pp. 573–589.

Barthes, Roland (1981), *Camera Lucida: Reflections on Photography*, New York: Hill and Wang.

Barthes, Roland (1983), *Empire of Signs*. Translated from French by Richard Howard, London: Jonathan Cape.

Barthes, Roland (2000), "Inaugural Lecture, Collège de France." In: Susan Sontag (ed.), *A Barthes Reader*, New York: Hill and Wang, pp. 457–478.

Carey, Peter (2005), *Wrong About Japan*, London: Faber & Faber.

Clifford, James (1988), *Predicament of Culture*, Cambridge: Harvard University Press.

Coppola, Sofia (2003), *Lost in Translation*, Tokyo: Elemental Films.

Crary, Jonathan (1988), "Modernising Vision." In: Hal Foster (ed.), *Vision and Visuality*, Seattle: Bay Press.

Elkins, James (1995), "Marks, Traces, *Traits*, Contours, *Orli*, and *Splendores*: Nonsemiotic Elements in Pictures," *Critical Inquiry*, 21 (4), pp. 822–860.

Elkins, James (1996), "What Do We Want Pictures to Be? Reply to Mieke Bal," *Critical Inquiry*, 22 (3), pp. 590–602.

Elkins, James (2003), *Visual Studies: A Skeptical Introduction*, New York: Routledge.

Jay, Martin (2002), "Cultural Relativism and the Visual Turn," *Journal of Visual Culture,* 1 (3), pp. 267–278.

Kerr, Alex (1996), *Lost Japan*, Oakland: Lonely Planet Publications.

Kracauer, Siegfried (1995), *The Mass Ornament: Weimar Essays*. Translated from German by Thomas Y. Levin. Cambridge: Harvard University Press.

McGovern, Sean (2004), "The Ryôan-ji Zen Garden: Textual Meanings in Topographical Form," *Visual Communication*, 3 (3), 344–359.

Manghani, Sunil (2003), "Adventures in Subsemiotics: Towards a New 'Object' and Writing of Visual Culture," *Culture, Theory and Critique*, 44 (1), 23–36.

Mitchell, W. J. (1994), *The Reconfigured Eye: Visual Truth in the Post-Photographic Era*, Cambridge: MIT Press.

Mitchell, W. J. T. (1994), *Picture Theory: Essays on Verbal and Visual Representation*, Chicago: University of Chicago Press.

Mitchell, W. J. T. (1996), "What do pictures 'really' want?," *October*, 77, pp.71–82.

Scott, Ridley (1982), *Blade Runner*, Los Angeles: The Ladd Company.

Shelton, Barrie (1999), *Learning from the Japanese City: West Meets East in Urban Design*, London: E & FN Spon.

Spivak, Gayatri Chakravorty (1988), "Can the Subaltern Speak?" In: Cary Nelson and Lawrence Grossberg (eds.), *Marxism and the Interpretation of Culture*, London: Macmillan.

Venturi, Robert, Scott Brown, Denise, & Izenour, Steven (1977), *Learning from Las Vegas: The Forgotten Symbolism of Architectural Form*, Cambridge: MIT Press.

Waley, Paul (1992), *Fragments of a City: A Tokyo Anthology*, Tokyo: The Japan Times.

Endnotes

1. In one recent article, there is an account of the "textual meanings in topographical form" of the ancient Ryôan-ji Zen garden (in Kyoto). It is a very good example of the kind of "labour of knowledge" Barthes stands against. The article in question demonstrates a good knowledge of the Zen garden, as well as Japanese culture and language in general. Thus on one level—at least to the uninitiated—it offers a useful introduction. However, what underpins its "examination" is a somewhat nullifying

"textual exegesis"—by the close it is stated "the Ryôan-ji garden as text sheds light on what was previously regarded as merely an aesthetic object and inevitably ineffable" (McGovern 2004, p. 357). For anyone who has sat before this garden, it will be patently obvious such remarks are entirely dispensable—in fact, it is precisely before a garden of this kind where you would hope to rid such "non-sense" from your mind!

2. It is important to note that Jay does not dismiss cultural specificity, but he does pitch against the rising trend for a cultural studies approach to visual culture, which sees everything in respect of cultural construction. In drawing upon James Clifford's *Predicament of Culture* (1988), Jay holds to the view that culture cannot have its boundaries drawn up. As a result "the idea that different cultures produce incommensurable views of the world cannot logically hold … Thus the strong argument for cultural determinism and incommensurability begins to waver." Instead, Jay is in favor of what Bruno Latour labels "relational relativism, rather than absolute relativism, an alternative that sees the world made up of hybrids, quasi-objects that include as much as they exclude" (Jay 2002, pp. 273, 274). In this light, any concerns about translating between cultures are seemingly misplaced. Indeed, as Latour asks: "How can one claim that worlds are untranslatable …when translation is the very soul of the process of relating?" (cited in Jay 2002, p. 274).

3. The title, *Camera Lucida* (Barthes 1981), suggests the antithesis of the dark room or box of the *camera obscura*—and indeed Barthes notes explicitly that "it is a mistake to associate Photography … with the notion of a dark passage (*camera obscura*). It is *camera lucida* that we should say" (Barthes 1981, p. 106). Yet, the front plate, a Polaroid image by Daniel Boudinet—which W. J. T. Mitchell suggests could be "read" as "an emblem of the unreadability of photography"—demonstrates more the optical aperture of the *camera obscura* (and is not a light room at all). It shows, as Mitchell describes, "a veiled, intimate boudoir, simultaneously erotic and funereal, its tantalizingly partial revelation of light gleaming through the cleavage in the curtains like the secret at the centre of a labyrinth." From a reader's perspective, we might well think of ourselves still in the darkness, the ray of light an invitation for us to lift the curtain—to go out the window even. As Mitchell puts it, "if there is a *camera lucida* in this image it resides beyond the curtains of this scene, or perhaps in the luminous opening at its centre, an evocation of the camera's aperture" (Mitchell 1994, p. 302–303).

4. It is worth noting that in *Blade Runner* (Scott 1982), the image inquiry does indeed lead (us on) to this kind of critical disclosure "before the discovery" of detail and meaning. Replicants are *given* their own private photographs as a means to "authenticate" their artificial memories; and since we take photographs to be a "slice" of history (with the rays of *past* light retained in the crystals of photographic

paper), these images act as *aide-mémoire*, though in this case relating to an *invented* memory, or at least to someone else's memories. What this comes to mean is that as Deckard faces up to the "reality" of the photograph loaded into the Esper machine, he is equally (though he might not actually know it) facing up to his own potential "empty" significance—indeed, the potentially catastrophic circumstance in which (as "we" the spectator begin to realize) Deckard, the admirable hunter of replicants, might himself be a replicant. In *Blade Runner* (Scott 1982), then, the more we get to see the more we have room to doubt; the photographs playing "host" to what Siegfried Kracauer describes as "the go-for-broke game of the historical process;" a game that ultimately shows "the valid organisation of things remains unknown" (Kracauer 1995, pp. 62–63). Thus, in piecing together various images, the dilemma is—as Deckard himself may have become aware of—we might well end up with nothing . . . Or, put another way, as W. J. T. Mitchell supposes, "What pictures want in the last instance, then, is simply to be asked what they want, with the understanding that the answer may well be, nothing at all" (Mitchell 1995, p. 82).

5.   Japanese saying: "A hundred hearings does not equal one seeing", which is analogous to "a picture is worth a thousand words".

6.   Criticism can and has been levelled at this film for its representation of Japan and its people. Nevertheless, going beyond the comedy that arises out of moments of mistranslation or cultural incomprehension, there is perhaps more to be gained in appreciating its representations as held in inverted commas—to isolate, as Barthes would suggest, "a certain number of features," to enable one "to "entertain" the idea of an unheard-of system" (Barthes 1983, p. 3). It is also worth mentioning, additional footage that comes with the DVD version of the film provides useful insight into its making. Pertinent to my discussion here, a revealing moment comes in the filming of one of the key comedy scenes. The scene, in question, involves a Japanese director desperately trying to coach the American movie star for his performance in a whiskey commercial. The result is a terrible series of confusions as a result of mistranslations and cultural misunderstandings. Yet, the documenting of this film shoot shows the real (American *and* Japanese) film crew calmly and harmoniously making this scene, with director's instructions being issued in both English and Japanese.

Words Upon the Windowpane: Image, Text, and Irish Culture

Luke Gibbons

> The history of [Ireland] does not form itself into a picture, but remains only a huge blot — an indiscriminate blackness, which the human memory cannot charge itself with . . .
>
> – Thomas Carlyle

In 1939 the critic Gwynn published an article calling for a new initiative in Irish art: "Wanted: An Irish Millet" (Gwynn 1939). What is unusual about this plea is not just its belated call for a realist movement, but its failure to address a more basic question, why were there no figures of Millet's or Courbet's stature in nineteenth-century, or indeed, twentieth-century Irish art? The problem had not to do with the absence of creative energies in Irish culture—the literary revival and its aftermath projected a powerful Irish presence onto the world literary stage out of proportion to its small population or its political and economic importance. Nor had it to do with a lack of suitable social milieu: Ireland, like France, was a country with a predominantly Catholic peasant population, and Millet's celebrated picture of *The Angelus* (1857) was almost as popular as images of the Sacred Heart in Irish rural cottages. The difficulty at the aesthetic level would rather appear to be with the discourse of *realism* itself, with the demand that art hold the mirror faithfully up to nature. The realist movement in mid-nineteenth-century France borrowed its sense of purpose and democratic vision from the 1848 revolutions, which conferred a new dignity on the laboring poor. By contrast, the Irish rural poor in 1848 were staring into the abyss, in the midst of the Great Famine, which removed almost half the population through starvation, disease, or emigration. Not for the first time, the exaltation of art came up against the limits of representation: "the truth is too strong for fiction," wrote the novelist Maria Edgeworth of the grim realities of Irish life, "and on all sides pulls it asunder" (Edgeworth 1821, p. 350)

How does one represent the unrepresentable? It may be that one hundred years was not such a considerable time lag after all for Irish culture to "catch up" with an uncompromising realism, for even as late as 1945, the Irish government was unable to commemorate the centenary of the Great Famine—to name the unnameable. Other political anniversaries were officially acknowledged during this period, but the Great Famine was still too painful to look at nature or, for that matter, history in the eye. This may help us to understand why its traumatic memory left so little in the way of great prose works or paintings akin to Primo Levi's accounts of the Holocaust, Frederick Douglas's slave narratives in the United States, or Goya's demented visions of the horrors of war.

It may be that the calamity of the Great Famine was articulated ultimately not at the level of "content," in the sense of any particular great work directly addressing the catastrophe, but at the level of "form," precisely in the resistance to realism that Gwynn considered a major shortcoming of the Irish visual—and literary—imagination. Lawrence Langer, in his work *The Holocaust and the Literary Imagination* (1975, p. 43), argues that "to establish an order of reality in which the unimaginable becomes imaginatively acceptable exceeds the capacities of an art devoted entirely to verisimilitude," or an aesthetic of realism. It is only through *dis*figuration, rather than the ordering illusions of mimetic art, that these disturbing areas of experience are rendered intelligible—that is, insofar as they make sense at all.

Hence, for example, the wayward fictions of James Joyce, Samuel Beckett, and Flann O'Brien in Irish literature, in which even the most scrupulous naturalistic details seem unable to escape the "nightmare of history" or the indeterminacies of identity. It is common to attribute the innovative narrative strategies of these writers to their encounter with the European avant-garde on the grounds that they had no Irish precursors, given the absence of a strong tradition in the nineteenth-century Irish novel. But although there may have been no outstanding realist works of the caliber of *Middlemarch: A Study of Provincial Life* (Eliot 1871) or *Madame Bovary* (Flaubert 1857), the Irish novel did attain an international reputation through the aberrant gothic genre, through displaced national tales of terror—such as Charles Maturin's *Melmoth the Wanderer* (1820), which enjoyed cult status among writers such as Honoré de Balzac Balzac and Charles Baudelaire, Sheridan Le Fanu's *Uncle Silas* (1864), or, most famous of all, *Dracula* (1897), written by the Dublin born ex-civil servant Bram Stoker.[1] These novels are plagued with anxieties about origins and destinations that extend to their modes of narration, making it all but impossible to achieve the closure and certainty afforded by the conventions of classical realism.

The resistance to realism in Irish culture, then, has nothing to do with a "Celtic" disposition to "react against the despotism of fact," as Matthew Arnold's stereotype would have it, or with an Irish aptitude for fantasy and superstition, but it is rather rooted in what Seamus Deane calls "the brute facts of history" (see Arnold 1867; Dean

1985). For almost every fifty years since the consolidation of colonial rule under Queen Elizabeth in 1603, with its overt ideology of genocide and expropriation, the Irish body politic has been exposed to successive shocks and convulsions, whether in the form of the Cromwelliam atrocities of the mid-seventeenth century, the Williamite Wars of the 1690s, the horrific famine of 1740/1741 (which may have killed more, proportionately, than the Great Famine a century later), the 1798 rebellion, the Great Famine of 1845–1851, the Land War of the 1880s, the War of Independence of 1916–1922, or the more recent Troubles, which broke out in Northern Ireland in 1968.[2]

The chronic instability and strife that prevented the development of a strong realist aesthetic also militated against the mimetic powers of the image, and the cultivation of the visual arts, in Ireland. This is to say that even if the material conditions of education, patronage, and the art market were favorable (which they decidedly were not under colonial rule), there is still a sense in which the available styles and protocols of painting would have been unable to render the extremes of Irish life. The problem is not unlike that which faces contemporary artists or filmmakers struggling to visualize the Holocaust. Throughout the nine and one-half hours of *Shoah* (1985), Claude Lanzmann's anguished epic on the concentration camps, there is a continual refusal to show archival or actuality footage, as if somehow these graphic records could not be used without risking the nostalgia and aesthetic pleasure that comes from grainy *cinema verite*. Likewise with painting—the seduction of the surface and the refinement of form are inimical to the disordering of the senses and the emotional excess produced by catastrophe and pain. As the postmodern critic and theorist J. F. Lyotard argues:

> Painting is doomed to imitate models, and to figurative representations of them. But if the object of art is to create intense feelings in the addressee of works, figuration by means of images is a limiting constraint on the power of emotive expression since it works by recognition. In the arts of language, particularly in poetry . . . where certain researches into language have free rein, the power to move is free from the verisimilitudes of figuration. (Lyotard 1989, p. 205).

To place this argument in its historical context, Lyotard invokes the aesthetic concept of the *sublime*, which set itself the paradoxical task of "bearing pictorial or otherwise expressive witness to the inexpressible," to contradictory feelings of "pleasure and pain, joy and anxiety, exaltation and depression." Though first promulgated in the eighteenth century, the sublime, according to Lyotard, "is the only mode of artistic sensibility to characterize the modern." Having disappeared from the lexicon of art for more than a century, Lyotard contends that it resurfaced as a mode of figuration in the avant-garde work of the American abstract artist Barnett Newman in the late 1940s. Since its reemergence, the sublime, as a liminal form of experience that addresses itself to the "inexpressible" and the "unrepresentable," has been variously invoked by critics and cultural historians as the most appropriate category (or anticategory) for mapping out the terrors of the twentieth century, and its historical antecedents—the Holocaust (Lyotard 1989),[3] "the slave sublime" and the millions who died in the middle passage between Africa and America (Gilroy 1993), the depredations of British colonialism in India under the East India Company (Suleri 1992), or the intimations of nuclear catastrophe in our own time (Ferguson 1984; Wilson 1981), regrettably still with us even after the demise of the Cold War. "It remains to the art historian," Lyotard adds, "to explain how the word sublime reappeared in the language of a Jewish painter from New York during the forties," noting, in a significant aside, that Newman had "read Edmund Burke's *Inquiry* [*into . . . the Sublime and the Beautiful* (1757)] and criticized what he saw as Burke's over 'surrealist' description of the sublime work" (Lyotard 1989, p. 199).

But if it is incumbent on art historians to explain the reemergence of the sublime in the post–World War II period, the task facing Irish cultural critics and historians is to explain how this mythos of terror was formulated in the first place in eighteenth-century Ireland, in the tormented aesthetic writings of the young Burke (1729–1797). According to Burke:

> Whatever is fitted in any sort to excite the ideas of pain, and danger, that is to say, whatever is in any way terrible, or is conversant about terrible objects, or operates in a manner analogous to terror, is a source of the sublime; that is, it is productive of the strongest emotion which the mind is capable of feeling (Burke 1958, p. 39).

Whereas French contemporaries of Burke, such as Denis Diderot and Rousseau, looked to clarity and transparency as the ruling principles of art, Burke instead argued that darkness, obscurity, and indistinctness are capable of the most powerful aesthetic emotions:

> It may be observed that very polished languages, and such as are praised for their superior clearness and perspicuity, are generally deficient in strength. The French language has that perfection, and that defect. Whereas the oriental tongues, and in general the languages of most unpolished people, have a great force and energy of expression (Burke 1958, p. 176).

"A clear idea," he added, "is therefore another name for a little idea." Having assailed the very basis of the metaphor of "enlightenment," Burke went on to displace *sight* from its preeminent position among the senses, arguing that words were superior to images in negotiating the terrors of the sublime. Employing reasoning very close to that used by Claude Landsman to justify the exclusion of "realistic" archival footage from *Shoah* (1985), Burke writes that "when painters have attempted to give us clear representations of . . . terrible ideas, they have I think almost always failed; insomuch that I have been at a loss, in all the pictures I have seen of hell, whether the painter did not intend something ludicrous." By contrast:

> there are many things of a very affecting nature, which can seldom occur in the reality, but the words which represent them often do; and thus they have an opportunity of making a deep impression and taking root in the mind, whilst the idea of the reality was transient; and to some perhaps never really occurred in any shape, to whom it is very affecting, as war, death, famine, &c. (Burke 1958, p. 174).

The mention of "famine" is salutary here, for it may be that Burke's disturbing aesthetic of the sublime was not simply proleptic where the Great Famine of 1845–1851 was concerned but may have resulted from his own experience of famine as a young boy raised in the Cork countryside in 1740/1741, where the combined failure of both the potato and cereal crops led to the death of one-third of the population of the county. These are the dark formless shadows on the landscape, "the indiscriminate blackness," which provoked Thomas Carlyle's exasperated statement, quoted in the epigraph, to the effect that Irish history does not lend itself to the clarity and coherence of pictorial representation.

1

For Burke, a purely pictorial medium, devoid of "extra visual" trappings having to do with language, time, and narrative, could not do justice to the unimaginable suffering of war, death, and famine. His aesthetics may be seen, therefore, as an attempt to reverse the radical divergence between word and image, which, according to Michel Foucault, presided over the development of Western painting in the modern period. "What is essential," writes Foucault of this trend, "is that verbal signs and visual representations are never given at once. An order always hierarchizes them, running from the figure to discourse or from discourse to figure" (Foucalt 1982, pp. 32–33). If, in the light (or shadow) of Burke's aesthetics, we turn to the contemporary work of the photographic and installation artist Willie Doherty, we encounter a series of highly wrought meditations on word and image, and time and space, in the context of the recurring terror of the conflict in Northern Ireland.

Clarity is the first casualty in Doherty's melancholy images of the politically contested terrain of his native Derry. In a series of photographs of the nationalist Bogside district in the city, "Fog Ice/Last Hours of Daylight" (1985) and "Undercover/Unseen" (1985), we encounter a menacing atmospheric haze that is far removed from the romantic mists of the Celtic twilight. The images, paradoxically, seek to represent what cannot be seen. In the artist's own words:

> Just as important in these photographs is what is not shown — the things you can't see here are the things that impinge most on your life. The idea that you are being watched or the idea that surveillance takes place daily. You can't photograph these, they're not public . . . You can only photograph something that is physically in front of you but you suggest them as a psychological state . . . (Fox 1986).

There is a persistent ambiguity in these images over what it means to escape visibility. On the one hand, it signifies an escape from the all-seeing eye of military intelligence—the word SHROUDING overlaid on one of the images contrasts with SURVEILLANCE on another image. If, as Paul Virilio maintains, war in an era of advanced electronic technology is less a theater of operations than a (battle)field of vision, then invisibility is vital as a strategy of resistance or even as a means of maintaining one's identity. "The problem of knowing who is the subject of the state and war," wrote Maurice Merleau-Ponty, "will be of exactly the same kind as the problem of knowing who is the subject of perception" (Virilio 1989, p. 2). As Virilio points out, however, this also applies to the military, who have even greater resources at their disposal to exploit the logistics of perception. Hence the words UNDERCOVER: BY THE RIVER and UNSEEN: TO THE BORDER inscribed on another set of contrasting images of the rural landscape leave us in doubt over who exactly is unseen—the forces of insurgency or those of counter insurgency. This suggests that instead of being a defense against oppression, invisibility can turn into an extension of it, as is borne out by the word STIFLING hovering over the envelope of smog during "the last hours of daylight" in the Bogside.

Though the landscape appears empty in the rural scenes, it bears all the signs of inhabited—or occupied—territory: the tell-tale tracks in the frost, the path beaten through the waste ground. One of the distinguishing features of the darker forms of Romanticism associated with the sublime in Irish culture is that landscape is no longer scenery, a source of visual pleasure, but is a menacing presence, concealing as much as it reveals. In the documentary film *Picturing Derry* (Fox 1985), a member of a Derry photography group recounts how she answered objections over the lack of scenery in a photography exhibition they brought to England: the difficulty with scenery, she pointed out, was if the landscape is photographed.

> We don't know what's behind the trees and bushes, and little did I know that two years later my husband was to be shot dead by the British army and the RUC [Royal Ulster Constabulary], and they lay in wait for him

behind bushes and trees, and he was shot in a really scenic site . . . . That is what scenery means to us . . . when you take a photograph, you don't think it is lovely scenery, you think it is nice, okay, but you ask what is happening on it.

To ask what is happening on the landscape is to narrativize it, to open it up to competing stories and interpretations of what happened. In Doherty's 1993 installation "30th January 1972," the cityscape of Derry on the fateful day of Bloody Sunday, in which fourteen innocent civilians were shot dead on an anti-internment march by British soldiers, becomes a contested site of memory and denial.[4] Slides are apprehended from different vantage points in an enclosure, with tunnel-like exits and entrances. In one case, a slide can be viewed on both sides of a wall, which leaves it difficult to determine whether we are inside or out. The slide in question depicts an insignificant street scene, until we learn that it depicts Glenfada Park, where many of the killings took place. The other slide projected on the inside walls of the enclosure is composed of a blurred still from TV news footage of the march that forms the main interior slide. This is a still life in more ways than one, for some of the marchers visible in the shot may have been dead within an hour. None of this is conveyed pictorially, for the images do not speak for themselves. Instead, our viewing is circumscribed by sound tracks with multiple voices that combine both the shock of the actual moment— "Get an ambulance!"—with memories that emanate like echoes from the back of the enclosure—"I think I was the last person he spoke to," "Bloody Sunday will always be Derry." It is as if the past interpenetrates the present, memory itself being caught in a freeze-frame.

The power of popular memory to instill recollections of events that were not even personally experienced is brought out vividly in Margo Harkin's television documentary *The Bloody Sunday Murders* (1992). The young narrator, Maureen Shiels, announces to camera at the outset that even though she was only two years old at the time "like everybody else in the community, I live with the memory of it. For the relatives of the dead, the memory is as raw as it ever was." What is unusual about the film is that the more familiar black-and-white television archival footage from the outbreak of the Troubles is counterpointed by the bleached color of home movies. Contesting the official narratives that exonerated the parachute regiment ("Army can be Proud" proclaims a London *Daily Express* headline intercut with eyewitness accounts), these plaintive, mute images function almost like a sound track, conveying the kind of personal testimony normally reserved for the human voice. The images are important, not just for what they show, but for the narratives they trigger in a community, the kind of images, as Doherty puts it in a similar context, that take much longer to reveal themselves than more arresting photojournalistic pictures, which yield up their meanings at a glance.

The extent to which images, in certain contexts, acquire the grain of the voice, is evident in one sequence in *Picturing Derry* (Fox 1985), in which a woman, whose son was shot on Bloody Sunday, is interviewed about her memories of the Troubles. As she goes through her photograph albums with the interviewer, it becomes clear that one of the albums, marked "The Hunger Strikers" is clearly set apart for political memorabilia. When she opens the family album, there are the usual snapshots of christenings, weddings, and so on, but these personal mementoes are also interspersed with photographs of Bloody Sunday and of photographs of the hunger strike campaign taking place in the streets of Derry. It is as if the public domain infiltrates private life, infusing political allegiances with the resonances and emotional charge of personal affections. In Stephen Burke's memorable short film *After 68* (Burke 1993), the diary-type voiceover of a teenage girl, Frieda, imparts to the public images of the escalating struggle in the early years of the Northern conflict a deeply felt, almost self-revelatory quality. "Someone once said that the proper place for politics is in the streets," the young narrator says at one point; however, no sooner has she finished the sentence than her activist mother enters the living room, bloodied from a street riot. Frieda is still apolitical and withdraws into her personal space by embarking on a relationship with the handsome Tommy Halpin. The "outside" world of politics seems to operate at one remove from her life and is relayed primarily through media images and broadcasts, but it inexorably impinges on the domestic arena as a pitched battle between nationalists and the British army spills in through the front door of their house. Frieda and her mother are forced to leave the war zone and retreat temporarily to the countryside; however, when they return, a young family is squatting in their terraced house, and they have no home to which to go. Even though political and public events are recast in the film through the intimacy of the voice, the film ultimately suggests that there is perhaps no secluded intimate or personal sphere in a political community so riven with conflict. As Frieda and her mother leave their "home" for the last time, they are stopped at an Irish Republican Army (IRA) checkpoint and through the mask of one of the gunmen, Frieda detects the face of her erstwhile boyfriend.

2

The interpenetration of public and private in the Northern conflict is on a continuum with a blurring of the boundaries between culture and nature, and between inner life and the external world, in Irish culture. Inner or psychic states are not simply related to the external environment through analogy, as in the poetic figure of "pathetic fallacy," but are rather embedded in the natural world through the visceral mediation of the body. Discussing the historical absence of an appreciation of nature, in its Enlightenment or Romantic sense, in Irish culture, Dorinda Outram argues that the recognition of an independent "external" natural world was compromised because of its inextricable links with the body in Irish Catholicism (and, she might have added, with attitudes toward the land under colonial rule):

> The only element of this natural order which is routinely, even insistently, referred to, is the human body itself.... Concern with the control of bodily events has seemingly inevitably been accompanied by a screening out of any debate of man's control over, or active intervention in, the shaping of the natural order. That environmental issues have little or no place in debates recognised as politically crucial in Ireland today is a significant fact. Instead "the natural" is allowed a role in political culture only in the area of individual management of the body (Outram 1986, p. 47).

The fact that control of the flesh was particularly directed at the female body made the liaison between woman and nature more intimate, and more estranged, in Irish culture.

In Jim Sheridan's film *The Field* (1990), the main protagonist, the Bull McCabe is threatened with dispossession of his property by an outsider and protests bitterly that his right to the family farm is grounded not in law or market forces but in a maternal birthright that extends beyond lineal descent. His mother collapsed in the field, he recalls, while rushing to bring in the hay before rains, but rather than going to her assistance, the Bull and his father in their manic obsession with the land decided to leave her there until the hay was brought in. The maternal body becomes commingled with the field itself, the sacrificial foundation of the farm and of the oedipal economy. This might be taken as a comment on the values that prevailed in the Irish countryside after the Great Famine, in the sense that those who were fortunate enough to survive acquired more smallholdings by almost literally walking on the bodies of their previous occupants. "They must be buried all around us," the priest remarks ruefully in *The Field* (1990), explaining to the visiting American who proposes to purchase the Bull's land why the Irish cling so tenaciously to the land.

The deconstruction of this fraught relationship between earth and flesh, and in particular between landscape and the female body, has been a recurrent feature of recent art by Irish women. In Kathy Prendergast's *Stack* (1989), the dense physicality of a 2.7-meter-high work made of cloth, paint, and twine resembles a cutaway segment of the Irish earth, the layers of fabric packed tightly on one another, simulating the disparate histories threaded through the "strata" of soil. This is a view of what is below the surface, and it reveals the unacknowledged role of women's work—the painstaking, repetitive labor of the textile maker—in fashioning the contours of the landscape. This desire to explore the hidden foundations of the landscape is taken up in the *Body Map* (1983) series of drawings, which parody the use of cartographic conventions to map the anatomy of the landscape/body. Meticulous drawings of the female body are shown in cross section, as if undergoing exploration by pioneers or mineralogists. The various parts of the body are labeled meticulously, the names indicating where conquests of the virgin territory are likely to prove productive or dangerous—the breasts denoting volcanic mountains, the abdomen a desert with the navel as a crater, the womb an underground cavern, and so on. Various idiosyncratic projects designed to "control" the landscape are then outlined in pseudoscientific prose accompanying the images, proposing, for example, that water found below the "crater" be diverted and stored underneath the "mountains," where, having quenched the fires, it can then be pumped through the "volcanic ducts" to fertilize the plains.

The awesome power and energy of the volcano entered the Romantic lexicon in the eighteenth century as an emblem of male prowess, of the heroic sublime in all its immense potential in the public sphere. What is striking in recent Irish woman's art is the extent to which the figure of the volcano has been recuperated for a version of the female sublime. In Cecily Brennan's work from 1991, based on Icelandic landscapes, the lesions and plasmalike movements of volcanic soil are refigured in terms of a woman's experience of gestation and childbirth, the inner earthquake that convulses the maternal body. The sublime is negotiated through the innermost recesses of the female body, inscribing the most intimate and "domestic" concerns in a public space (the wilderness of "the Arctic sublime") normally reserved for heroic, male endeavor.

The plotting of the maternal body in public space is set in the traumatized landscapes of the Great Famine in Alanna O'Kelly's installation, "The Country Blooms, a Garden and a Grave" (1992). The priest's remark in *The Field* (1990), that "they are buried all around us," is visually evoked in a volcano-shaped promontory on a deserted beach in County Mayo, Teampall Dumnach Mhor [Church of the Great Sandbank]. Though the mound dates back to the early Christian era, it became a site of mourning in the nineteenth century when it was used as a mass grave during the Great Famine. The dissolution of the body in the landscape is worked into an adjoining image of a woman's hands, the clay-caked fingers resembling the ridges of "lazy beds" where potatoes were planted before the Great Famine. When, in the following image, the hands are upturned, it transpires that they are empty and are in fact supplicating for food. The contours of the mass grave on the shore undergo a similar transformation, echoing the shape of the maternal breast which, in a video sequence, is shown expressing milk underwater. As the milk emanates from the breast in what seems like slow motion, it comes to resemble the emission of smoke from a smoldering volcano, clouding the water. As in Kathy Prendergast's "exploration" series, the destructive force of the volcano is retrieved as a life principle, a source of hope rather than despair. Yet, as if the clouding of the image exemplifies the obscurity of the sublime, this vision of the lifegiving plenitude of the breast is itself offset by sound and the somnolent cadences of the female voice. Eerie, dirgelike cries of whales merge with a whispered litany of the dead and the wailing sounds of traditional Irish keening, in which the female voice resonates with the pain of mourning. It is as if the most incidental details of the landscape, or indeed everyday life, can trigger subterranean narratives of long-buried memories

Roland Barthes has suggested that in moments of trauma, images escape from the cultural codes of language and narrative and are forced back on their own purely optical devices (Barthes 1977, pp. 30–31). Shock and trauma jolt us out of the reassuring routines and habits to which culture accustoms us, inducing a kind of tableau effect that suspends the flow of language and meaning. We are stunned into silence with only images separating us from madness. In Ireland, however, it is culture itself that is in contention and the foundations that are at fault. Rather than acting as a shock absorber, tradition itself constitutes a threat that is capable of unleashing the unresolved narratives buried in language, custom, and popular memory. In times of stress, images recoil from the opticality envisaged by Barthes and are instead shadowed by "an indiscriminate blackness" of a past that will not go away. Visual representation breaks down and words, as Foucault puts it, hover in the vicinity of the frame,

> like an infinite murmur—haunting, enclosing the silence of figures, investing it, mastering it, extracting the silence from itself, and finally reversing it within the domain of things that can be named (Foucault 1982, p. 34).

Art, in these circumstances, offers cold comfort to the eye. In the aftermath of the peace process, Irish people have been enjoined repeatedly to draw a line over the past, but it may well be that the real difficulty in Irish culture is to draw the past at all.

References

Arnold, Matthew (1867), *On the Study of Celtic Literature*, London: Smith, Elder & Co.

Barthes, Roland (1977), "The Photographic Message." In: *Image – Music – Text*, translated by Stephen Heath, London: Fontana/Collins.

Bradshaw, Brendan (1989), "Nationalism and Historical Scholarship in Ireland," *Irish Historical Studies,* 26 (104), pp. 329–351.

Burke, Edmund (1757), *A Philosophical Enquiry into the Origin of Our Ideas of the Sublime and the Beautiful*, s.l: s.n. [J. T. Boulton ed., London: Routledge and Kegan Paul, 1958].

Burke, Stephen (1993), *After 68*, Derry and Londonderry: Mammoth Films.

Deane, Seamus (1985), *Celtic Revivals: Essays in Modern Irish Literature*, London: Faber.

Deane, Seamus (1994), "Land and Soil: A Territorial Rhetoric," *History Ireland*, 2 (1), pp. 31–34.

Edgeworth, Richard Lovell & Edgeworth, Maria (1821), *Memoirs*, Vol. 2, London: R. Hunter and Baldwin, Cradock and Joy.

Eliot, George (1871), *Middlemarch: A Study of Provincial Life*, Edinburgh and London: William Blackwood and Sons.

Ferguson, Frances (1984), "The Nuclear Sublime," Diacritics 14 (2) pp. 4–10.

Flaubert, Gustave (1857), *Madame Bovary*, Paris: Revue de Paris.

Foucault, Michel (1982), *This is Not a Pipe*. Translated from French by James Harkness, Berkeley: University of California Press.

Fox, David (1985), *Picturing Derry*, Derry: Faction Films.

Fox, David (1986), Interview in *Picturing Derry*, Derry: Faction Films.

Gilroy, Paul (1993), "'Not a Story to Pass On': Living Memory and the Slave Sublime." In: *The Black Atlantic: Modernity and Double Consciousness*, London: Verso.

Gwynn, Stephen (1939), "Wanted: An Irish Millet," *The Irish Digest*.

Harkin, Margo (1992), *The Bloody Sunday Murders*.

Howes, Marjorie (1992), "Misalliance and Anglo-Irish Tradition in Le Fanu's Uncle Silas," *Nineteenth-Century Literature*, 47 (2), pp. 164–186.

Langer, Lawrence (1975), *The Holocaust and the Literary Imagination*, New Haven: Yale University Press.

Lanzmann, Claude (1985), *Shoah*, Auschwitz: Historia.

Le Fanu, J. S. (1864), *Uncle Silas*, London: Richard Bentley.

Lyotard, Jean-François, "The Sublime and the Avant-Garde." In: Andrew Benjamin, (ed.) (1989), The Lyotard Reader, London: Blackwell Publishing.

Maturin, Charles Robert (1820), *Melmoth the Wanderer*, Edinburgh: Archibald Constable.

McCormack, W. J., "Irish Gothic and After, 1820–1945." In: Seamus Deane (ed.), (1981), *The Field Day Anthology of Irish Writing*, Vol. 2, Derry and London: Field Day Publications.

Norris, Christopher (1992), *Uncritical Theory: Postmodernism, Intellectuals and the Gulf War*, London: University of Massachusetts.

Outram, Dorinda (1986), "Negating the Natural: Or Why Historians Deny Irish Science," *The Irish Review* (1), pp. 45–49.

Sheridan, Jim (1990), *The Field*, Aasleigh: Granada Television.

Stoker, Bram (1897), *Dracula*, New York: W. R. Caldwell & Co.

Suleiri, Sara (1992), "Edmund Burke and the Indian Sublime." In: *The Rhetoric of English India*, Chicago: University of Chicago.

Virilio, Paul (1989), *War and Cinema*. Translated from French by Patrick Camillier, London: Verso.

Wilson, Rob (1981), "Towards the Nuclear Sublime: Representations of Technological Vastness in Postnuclear America." In: *The American Sublime: The Genealogy of a Poetic Genre*, Madison: University of Wisconsin Press.

Endnotes

1. For the argument that Irish gothic novels, even when set elsewhere, often represent displacements of Irish concerns, see McCormack (1991), Howes (1992), and Deane (1994).

2. According to Brendan Bradshaw, much recent Irish "revisionist" historiography is characterized by a systematic attempt to suppress precisely this "catastrophic" dimension in Irish history (see Bradshaw 1989).

3. In Christopher Norris's summary of Lyotard's recourse to aesthetic concepts in his discussion of the Holocaust, "the sublime would offer the most fitting analogy for an event which defies all forms of adequate representation, which reason... is totally unable to assimilate, and which therefore demands that we respond to its summons without falling back on established criteria or protocols of validating judgement" (Norris 1992, p. 76).

4. Internment without trial of more than 700 civilians and activists from the nationalist community was introduced on 9 August 1971.

A Visually-Oriented Literary Culture?

Kris Van Heuckelom

The influence of cultural mediation on the physiological process of seeing is a recurring topic in the field of visual studies. An example that is often given when discussing the proclaimed cultural variability of ocular experience is the difference between a Hellenic and a Hebraic approach to visual experience. Ancient Greece is said to be at the roots of the concept of sight as "being the noblest of the senses," whereas Jewish culture is usually linked to a tradition of iconoclasm and antirepresentationalism. The conventional wisdom holding that Judaism is indifferent or even hostile to the visual arts has, of course, been doubted, but it remains a fact that in the Jewish case, one can find a significant amount of prescriptive (i.e., religious) texts expressing a rather negative attitude toward visual experience and representation (see Olin 2001; Bland 2001). The reasons one culture or the other tends to evolve (or to represent itself) as rather visually or nonvisually oriented are, however, not always easy to discern. In this historical survey, I will present a case study that focuses on the highly ambiguous status of visual practices in Polish culture. I will not only critically discuss some of the elements that are likely to have played a significant role in the historical development of Poland (representing itself) as a predominantly literary or verbal culture but will also try to show to what extent the concept of visual literacy might be useful when discussing the cultural variability of visual experience.

The ideal starting point for a critical discussion of the ambiguous status of the visual in Polish culture is a remarkable essay published in Paris by the Polish art and literary critic Julian Klaczko (1825–1906).[1] Being a regular contributor to *La Revue des Deux Mondes/Review of the Two Worlds*, the most influential Parisian review at the time, Klaczko was known for his provocative opinions on both political and cultural affairs. His essay, entitled "Sztuka Polska"/ "Polish Art," (1857) aimed at discussing the state of Polish art in the second half of the nineteenth century and at answering the question in what direction Polish art should evolve in the decades and centuries to come. Generally speaking, Klaczko began with two basic facts:

1. the poor and belated development of the visual/plastic arts in Poland

2. the high status that was traditionally assigned in Polish culture to literature

Or to put it in Klaczko's own words:

> Nie szperajmy w pergaminach za antenatami naszego rzeźbiarstwa i malarstwa, których nigdy nie było, ale umiejmy szczycić się i godnie wywiązać z tego prawdziwego szlachectwa, które nam w pięknym świecie ideału wielka nasza wyrobiła Poezja! (Klaczko 1961, p. 48).
> [Let us not sniff with our noses in old parchments to find the precursors of our sculpture and painting, because they have never existed, on the contrary, let us take pride in the true nobility that has been produced by our Poetry, in the beautiful world of ideals.]

From these two facts, Klaczko drew the following rather provocative assumptions:

1. historically speaking, at the roots of Polish culture lies a *sui generis* "verbocentrism"

2. as a consequence of this "verbocentrism," for Polish artists, it makes no sense whatsoever to try to be creative in the domain of the visual/plastic arts

Klaczko's essay gets very interesting the moment he attempts to provide a reasonable explanation for this proclaimed "verbocentric" character of Polish culture. Confronted with the obvious absence of normative religious concepts that could have been—as in the Jewish example—at the roots of the Pole's preference for the word, Klaczko resorts to an explanation of an ethnic nature. Obviously inspired by various theories of Pan-Slavism and Slavophilia that were in vogue in nineteenth-century eastern Europe, the author of "Polish Art" (Klaczko 1961 [1857]) refers to a presumed etymological link between the common Slavic ethnonym *Słowianie* [Slavs] and the phonetically similar stem *słowo* [word]. Following Klaczko's interpretation, the word *Słowianie* [Slavs] should actually be read and understood as "ludy Słowa" [people of the Word]. The author of *Polish Art* formulated his arguments in the following way:

> Dźwięk i słowo to są jedynie wcielenia dla polskiego i słowiańskiego ducha naturalne, nie wymuszone i prawdziwe, jedyne, które lud u nas zrozumieć, a masy uznać i uczcić są w stanie. … Słowianie, jesteśmy i możemy tylko być mistrzami Słowa! … Nie pędzłem i dłutem, lecz krzyżem a mieczem zwyciężała Polska od wieków (Klaczko 1858 pp. 44, 49, 69).

> [The sound and the word are for the Polish and Slav spirit the only
> natural, unimposed and true embodiment, the sole which our people can
> understand and our masses are capable of recognizing and appreciating .
> . . As Slavs, we are and can be only masters of the Word! . . . For centuries,
> Poland has won victories not by means of the paintbrush and chisel but
> with the cross and sword.]

Klaczko's arguments are, of course, insufficient or even incorrect on several levels.
First of all, the etymological interpretation of *Słowianie* as proposed in "Polish Art"
appears to be highly doubtful, although some linguists are still attracted by the idea
of linking the Slavic ethnonym semantically to the stem *słowo*.[2] Roman Jakobson, for
instance, has claimed that there is sufficient linguistic evidence in the Old Russian
language to maintain the presumed etymological link between *Słowianie* and *słowo* (see
Jakobson 1959). Jakobson refers to an argument that has often been used in support of
the interpretation of *Słowianie* as "people of the Word"—that is, the presumed semantic
link between *Słowianie* and the ethnonym *Niemcy* [mute people]. The word *Niemcy* was
used by the Slavs to refer to neighboring German tribes who could "not speak"—that is,
whose language was incomprehensible for the Slavs.

On a more general level, it is obvious that Klaczko employs a highly static and
essentialist concept of cultural identity, which inevitably leads to all kinds of unjustified
generalizations. As such, Klaczko's claim of Slavic "verbocentrism" is a typical Romantic
construct that relies on the presumed existence of some kind of common Slavic soul
or Slavic spirituality. Actually, Klaczko was not the first person to observe a neat link
between the proclaimed Polish preference for the word and the Slavic roots of the Poles.
Some fifteen years earlier, similar "Slavophilic" ideas had been expressed by the Polish
"national poet" Adam Mickiewicz, one of the main representatives of Polish Romantic
literature. In the years 1840–1844, the emigré writer Mickiewicz held the first chair of
Slavic literatures at the Collège de France in Paris and as such, he gave several series
of lectures devoted to issues of Slavic languages and cultures. In one of his lectures, in
which he discussed the common roots of Slavic culture, Mickiewicz referred to the poor
development of the visual arts in the Slavic part of Europe and explained this fact in the
following way:

> On comprendra maintenant pourquoi les Slaves n'ont pas jusqu'à présent
> cherché à faire de l'art plastique. Quel besoin auraient-ils de courir après
> des copies, puisqu'ils possèdent tout entier l'organe qui les rend capables
> de voir les originaux? Ces souvenirs du monde invisible que l'on taille
> en marbre, que l'on coule en bronze, et que l'on attache à la toile pour les
> préserver de l'oubli, le peuple slave les conserve tous vivants. Ce ne sont
> pas pour lui des souvenirs, c'est de la réalité, c'est de l'actualité. Le peuple

passe sa vie à raconter, à chanter les événements qui se déroulent sous la terre, dans les airs et au ciel. C'est pour n'avoir pas compris les merveilles de cette foi vivante des Slaves, que certains civilisateurs modernes croyaient rendre un grand service à ces pays en y transportant quelques statues et quelques tableaux. (Mickiewicz 1914, pp. 271–272).

[One can comprehend why up to now the Slavs have not engaged in the plastic arts. Apparently, the latter were never their vocation. Why should they compete for copies when they possess, in its full glory, an organ with whose aid they can see the originals? Those reminiscences of the invisible world that others, fearing that they might lose them, hew out of stone, cast from bronze, and place on canvas, the Slavs store alive. For the Slaves, they are not mere memories—it is reality, it is the actual world. The people live their life telling and singing about the things that happen beneath the ground, in the air and in heaven. It is because of the fact that they did not understand the marvels of this living Slavic faith that certain modern civilizers thought that they would do the Slavs a great favor by bringing them some statues and paintings.]

An unavoidably weak element in both Klaczko's and Mickiewicz's exposé is their provocative and exaggerated statement that up to the nineteenth century, Poland had not engaged at all in the visual arts. In fact, at that time, relatively little was known about the history and development of Polish visual arts from the Middle Ages to the nineteenth century. In the twentieth century, detailed art historical research was to bring to light a surprisingly varied tradition of Polish plastic artifacts.[3] Actually, Klaczko's essay appeared at a turning point in the history of Polish art. In the second half of the nineteenth century, Polish painting knew a rapid and exuberant development and began to produce its first "big names" (such as Jan Matejko and Stanisław Wyspiański). From this perspective, it should not be surprising that Klaczko's provocative essay provoked a lot of controversy and many vivid debates in circles of Polish artists and art critics.[4] Klaczko's statement turned out to have a catalyzing effect on the plastic output of Polish artists (as if they wanted to prove how terribly wrong he was), and soon afterward, both Klaczko's and Mickiewicz's discourse on the inherent Polish incapability to pursue the plastic arts was refuted by life itself. So, despite the fact that Polish culture in its artistic accomplishments seemed to have developed for a long time as a strongly verbally oriented culture, Klaczko's essentialist definition of Polish culture as "verbocentric" turned out to be a fallacy. Polish art and culture had their first huge "visual turn" in the second half of the nineteenth century and, during the twentieth century, several Polish artists have made significant contributions to Western visual culture—for example, in the domain of film and comics. This does not mean, of course, that the discourse on Poland as an inherently nonvisual culture entirely disappeared in the twentieth century.

Nowadays as well, there seems to exist a consensus that both on a quantitative and a qualitative level, Polish visual arts remained for a considerably long time in a minor position and that there still are people who tend to link this historical situation with some kind of chronic Polish lack of plastic or visual abilities. In the second part of this article, I will quote an interesting fragment from the postwar diaries of Gombrowicz, one of the main representatives of Polish Modernism, that links in a certain way to the nineteenth-century "Slavophilic" discourse of Klaczko and Mickiewicz.

The fact that Klaczko's peculiar analysis of the presumed Polish incapability to pursue the plastic arts turned out to be incorrect does not mean, of course, that his arguments are completely deprived of sense and do not deserve further attention and investigation. It seems appropriate at this point to make a clear distinction between two differing aspects of visual experience: visual sensitivity and visual literacy. On the one hand, it should be stressed that the fact that Polish culture has developed for a long time as a predominantly literary culture does not imply in any way an inherent lack of visual sensitivity. Convincing arguments against such a statement can be easily found in Polish literature. At least since the time of the Baroque era, Polish literature has been praised for its highly visualist and plastic character.[5] On the other hand, however, it seems appropriate and justified to say that Poland remained for a long time a culture of poor visual literacy—both on the level of image production and image reception. Moreover, there are elements indicating that this situation of relatively poor visual literacy and strong literary literacy played a significant role in the way Poles tended to represent or define themselves toward the outside world. In what follows, I will critically discuss some of the elements that are likely to have played a role in the historical development of Poland as a predominantly literary and verbal culture, and I will consider the way in which this evolution can be linked to Polish forms of self-representation and self-definition. In opposition to Klaczko and Mickiewicz, who attempted to find an essentialist explanation for the poor development of the visual arts in Poland (and who resorted to a vague concept of some kind of verbocentric Slavic spirituality), I will try to provide a functional approach toward the problem of visual practices in Poland. It should be obvious that I will be dealing with a complex mixture of historical circumstances and developments, which, of course, are often difficult to interpret in an unequivocal way.

First of all, it seems important to note that on a socioeconomic level, Poland remained for many ages a predominantly agrarian, gentry-dominated economy and did not develop a substantial middle class of traders and consumers. As such, Polish society remained for a long time—to quote a Polish historian—"inimical to the bourgeois ethic of thrift, investment, self-improvement, and discipline" that for many ages dominated the socioeconomic behavior of western Europe (Zamoyski 1999, p 37). In opposition to the development of a prosperous market for all kinds of image production in the mercantilistic and early capitalist societies of the West (for example, the Low Countries), the local demand in Poland for products of visual culture remained relatively low (see, for instance, Van der Stock 1998). Prestigious visual art projects were mostly initiated by the gentry, the Polish kings, or the Church and not by the middle class. Moreover, a serious crisis of Polish urban civilization in the seventeenth century meant that native artistic production kept within the bounds of provincialism and did not meet the academic standards indispensable for the skillful practicing of art. As a consequence, the vast majority of prestigious artistic and architectural projects were usually committed to foreign artists and craftsmen. This does not mean, of course, that there was absolutely no interest in the visual arts in Poland at the time. The fact that many artists came to Poland from elsewhere means that there was a market for art production, and these foreign-born artists sometimes created local centers that had a more or less lasting influence (in many cases, we find Polonized painters, whose ancestors had come from elsewhere). A second element that could indicate a certain interest in products of visual culture at the time is the considerable popularity of the emblemata genre and the *ut pictura poesis* tradition in Poland in the sixteenth and seventeenth centuries (see Pelc 2002). However, if we take a closer look at the local development of this genre in Poland, then we can see that the level of visual literacy of both Polish consumers and producers remained remarkably low. Polish emblemata editions were mostly inspired by foreign editions, usually by emblem books from the Low Countries and Italy. A highly significant example of the fact that the quality of these Polish emblemata was generally much lower than the quality of the graphic work in the original editions is provided by the book *Chwała z Krzyża/The Way of the Cross* (Hincza 1641), published in Krakow and based on an earlier Flemish edition (*Sacra Via Crucis*, van Haeften 1635; see Pelc 2002).[6] The fact, on the other hand, that Polish literary tradition was much stronger at that time is exemplified by the international renown Polish Neo-Latinist poet Maciej Kazimierz Sarbiewski (Matthias Casimirus Sarbievius) (1595–1640), who was one of the most popular European poets of his time and eventually received the honorary title of "the Christian Horace."[7]

Another element that is likely to have played a substantial role in the development of Poland as a culture of rather poor visual literacy and strong literary literacy is of a sociological nature. As I already mentioned, it was the Polish gentry [the *szlachta*], and not the middle class, who stood at the center of Polish social life. The Polish *szlachta* had plenty of political, social, and economic privileges, and at a certain point (sometime at the beginning of the Baroque era), it began to cultivate its superior position in Polish society in a rather peculiar and even megalomanic way. The nobility's feeling of superiority gradually grew into an all-embracing ideology, which is usually referred to as "sarmatism." The Sarmatians were thought to have been inhabitants of some lands situated in east central Europe that were occupied by the Polish Commonwealth in the sixteenth to eighteenth centuries. In the seventeenth century, the Polish *szlachta* started to claim that it descended from this legendary warrior people. The gentry's adaptation of Sarmatian culture had various features, which were all in some way tied up with the fact that in the seventeenth century, Poland was involved in a lot of wars, as a result of which the Polish *szlachta* had to spend a lot of its time on combat and warfare. Inspired by the Sarmatian myth, the Polish *szlachta* started to cultivate its military status of brave warriors and began to dress in an extravagant, oriental way. It treasured the craftsmanship and design of weaponry and horse trappings and savored the luxury of Ottoman textiles. Apart from that, the Sarmatian love of extravagance and ritual in everyday life was characterized by a pomposity both in oratory and narrative art. In times of peace, the gentry used to evoke its numerous military adventures abroad in long oral accounts. In this way, Polish Sarmatian culture even developed its own literary genre, the *gawęda* or *gawęda szlachecka* [gentry tale], which arose from the tradition of giving long speeches or telling colorful stories on pleasant occasions and at feasts. The most significant example of this highly developed culture of verbosity is the "spoken diaries" of Jan Chryzostom Pasek (1636–1701). As a young man of nineteen, Pasek enlisted in the Polish army and took part in several military campaigns. His famous *Memoirs* was— as Czesław Miłosz puts it—"written in his advanced age — or better: noted down, for they are mostly spoken tales which Pasek had probably told innumerable times before putting them on paper" (see Miłosz 1969, pp. 145–146). This Sarmatian tendency to verbosity also came to expression in the Polish political life at the time, namely, in the many heated political debates and quarrels that would later give the *sejm* (the Polish parliament) its legendary reputation. In several European languages, this Polish tendency to debate and quarrel endlessly turned into a stereotype (e.g. in Swedish [*Polsk riksdag*] and Dutch [*Poolse landdag*]). In later times, one can find numerous references to the Polish gentry's tradition of verbosity in the Polish "national poem" *Pan Tadeusz* [written by the aforementioned Mickiewicz (1834)].

Although the element of show was very important in the Polish gentry's Sarmatian way of life, relatively little money and energy were invested in the visual arts as such (a remarkable exception is the coffin portrait, one of the most original components of Polish Baroque art). In most cases, products of visual culture were closely linked to the warrior status of the Polish gentry. The *szlachta* invested mainly in movable goods and riches, which is to say clothing, jewelry, and arms. The noblemen were also very attached to their horses, which—as symbols of the *szlachta*'s warrior status—were dressed in fine trappings, covered with beautiful cloths, decorated with plumes and wings, and, on special occasions, dyed (Zamoyski 1999, p. 31). This Sarmatian way of life was characterized by a rather utilitarian approach to the fine arts but also by a preference for products of applied art. It is interesting to quote at this point a fragment from the diaries of Gombrowicz, one of the best-known Polish authors of the twentieth century. Gombrowicz used to call himself an "iconoclast," an opponent of the visual arts, and as such, he highly valued the Sarmatians' ambiguous attitude toward the fine arts. In his diaries, he linked this attitude to some kind of common Slavic distrust of the visual arts:

Gdyż nasz słowiański stosunek do spraw artyzmu jest bardziej luźny, mniej zaangażowaliśmy się w sztukę niż zachodnio-europejskie narody i stać nas na większą swobodę ruchów. ... Dziwi mnie, że malarze polscy nie próbują wyzyskać atutu, jakim na terenie sztuki jest polskość. Wieczniéż macie naśladować Zachód? Korzyć się przed malarstwem, jak Francuzi?... Uznaję ten rodzaj malarstwa, ale przecież on nie leży w naszej naturze, wszak tradycje nasze są inne, Polacy nigdy zbytnio nie przejmowali się sztuką, my skłonni byliśmy sądzić, że nie nos dla tabakiery, a tabakiera dla nosa... (Gombrowicz 1997, pp. 43–44).
[Our Slavic attitude toward artistic matters is lax. We are less involved in art than the Western European nations and so we can afford a freedom of movement.... I am amazed that Polish painters do no try to exploit their trump card, which is their Polishness, in art. Are you going to imitate the West forever? Prostrate yourselves before painting, like the French? ... I acknowledge this type of painting, but it is not in our nature because our traditions are different. Poles have never been especially concerned with art. We were inclined to believe that the nose was not for the snuff box but the snuff box for the nose... Gombrowicz 1988, pp. 25–26.]

On the other hand, this Sarmatian attitude toward art and culture undoubtedly served as a form of self-representation and self-definition. From the seventeenth century onward, the Poles started to ascribe to themselves an exclusive position in Western culture: they thought of themselves as guardians of Western Christianity and considered Poland to be the "antemurale christianitatis" [bulwark of Christianity]. This myth of being the defenders of Western culture gave the Poles the opportunity to differentiate themselves from western Europe—for example, in the field of art and culture. In an implicit way, this element of self-representation is present in the passage I quoted from Klaczko's "Polish Art " (1857), in which the author states that "for centuries, Poland had won victories not by means of the paintbrush and chisel but with the cross and sword": the main attributes of Polish culture, situated at the outskirts of European civilization, were not "the paintbrush and the chisel" but all kinds of objects and symbols that were connected in some way or the other with the military aspirations of the Polish gentry.

In later times, the predominantly verbal orientation of Polish culture was strongly reinforced by the political situation in which the country found itself in the nineteenth century. The period of the partitions (1772–1795) and Poland's long-lasting struggle for independence (1795–1918) led to the emergence of the "Romantic paradigm" in Polish social and cultural life. This Romantic–patriotic way of thinking tied the Poles' identity with their responsibilities to the national community and its struggle for independence. As the Polish scholars Maria Janion and Teresa Walas have shown, Polish literature came to play a central role in the development of this "Romantic paradigm" in Polish social life (see Janion 2000; Walas 2003). The Polish Romantic poets (including Mickiewicz, Juliusz Słowacki, and Zygmunt Krasiński) were considered to be preservers of the Polish selfhood and were called "prophets." Moreover, the preservation of the Polish nation and identity was strongly linked to the preservation of the Polish language. In one of the best-known Polish poems of the nineteenth century—Maria Konopnicka's *Rota* [Oath] (1908), which for some time fulfilled the function of the unofficial Polish anthem—most attention was paid to the preservation of the Polish language and the resistance against all attempts of Germanization. As such, Polish language and literature were considered to be the last bastion of Polishness that could never be taken over by foreign intruders. This "Romantic paradigm," stressing the writer's obligations toward society and reinforcing his central position in the country's social and cultural life, was revived during World War II and in the Communist period, when Poland found itself again under the governance of foreign invaders. According to the Communist regime, literature had to fulfill a key role in the revolutionary reshaping of society (as in socialist realism). The anticommunist opposition, on the contrary, used literature as one of the main instruments of moral resistance against the regime and turned writers into moral authorities. This long-lasting Romantic–patriotic style of thinking had a considerable influence on the Polish education system, which for a long time had been very strongly focused on the acquisition of literary literacy and, more specifically, on the teaching of Polish language and literature as cornerstones of Polish identity.

As a conclusion to this case study, it seems justified to state that in the case of Poland, we encounter a series of successive historical developments of a socioeconomic and a cultural nature that seem to have delayed the deployment of visual literacy and have strengthened the role of verbal creativity in the country's social and cultural life. It remains to be seen how long this historical situation will retain its topicality and relevance in the face of new sociological and technological developments. On the one hand, one might assume that the growing role of global visual culture in the twentieth century and the diminishing effect of the "Romantic paradigm" on Polish cultural life in the postcommunist period are likely to put an end to the traditional Polish discourse on "verbocentrism." On the other hand, one should keep in mind that Poland is a country with a strong nationalist and patriotic tradition, adhering to a rather static concept of cultural identity. For the moment, the Polish education system still seems to be strongly oriented toward the acquisition of verbal skills, and as far as I can judge, the field of visual studies is only marginally represented in the Polish academic and education worlds. Moreover, the growing deployment of visualization on a global scale is regarded by many—predominantly nationalist and Catholic—Poles as an enormous challenge, or to put it negatively, a danger to their culture. In the West, the proclaimed hegemony of capitalist-generated visual skills is often linked to the need for some kind of alternative or heterogeneous visuality, shaped by the artistic avant-garde. In Poland, however, the global deployment of visuality may lead, perhaps somewhat paradoxically, to a reinforcement of verbal literacy in the process of education. I will limit myself to one small, but nonetheless rather significant, example: a book published a few years ago by the

Polish bishop Adam Lepa titled *The Function of the Logosphere in Media Education* (2003). The author argues that the growing role of visual culture (or "iconosphere") may seriously threaten the Christian, patriotic, and national virtues of the Poles and, as such, he stresses the particular importance of the word (or "logosphere") in the process of education.

It is not at all clear to me how all this will evolve in the near or more distant future, so let me finish this historical survey by stating that in the Polish case, present and future sociological and technological developments will undoubtedly lead to a fascinating mixture of old and new—visual and verbal—practices and old and new—verbocentric and ocularcentric—discourses.

References

Backvis, Claude (1975), *Szkice o Kulturze Staropolskiej*, Warszawa: PIW.

Bland, Kalman P. (2001), *The Artless Jew: Medieval and Modern Affirmations and Denials of the Visual*, Princeton: Princeton University Press.

Brückner, Aleksander (1998), *Słownik Etymologiczny Języka Polskiego*, Warszawa: Wiedza Powszechna.

Gombrowicz, Witold (1988), *The Diary: 1953–1956*, Vol. 1. Translated from Polish by Lilian Vallee, Evanston: Northwestern University Press.

Gombrowicz, Witold (1997), *Dziennik 1953-1956*, Kraków: Wydawnictwo Literackie.

Hincza, Marcin (1641), *Chwała z Krzyża*, Kraków s. n..

Jakobson, Roman (1959), "Marginalia to Vasmer's Russian Etymological Dictionary (R-Ja)." In: *The International Journal of Slavic Linguistics and Poetics*, 1/2, pp. 265–278.

Janion, Maria (2000), *Do Europy: Tak, Ale Razem z Naszymi Umarłymi*, Warszawa: Sic!

Lepa, Adam (2003), *Funkcja Logosfery w Wychowaniu Do Mediów*, Łódź: Archidiecezjalne Wydawnictwo Łódzkie.

Klaczko, Julian (1857), "Sztuka Polska." In: *Wiadomości Polskie* (Paryż), 21/23/41.

Klaczko, Julian (1961), "Sztuka Polska", reprinted in: *Z dziejów Polskiej Krytyki i Teorii Sztuki*, Vol. 2, Warszawa: PWN.

Konopnicka, Maria (1908), *Rota*, s.l.: s.n.

Mickiewicz, Adam (1834), *Pan Tadeusz: Czyli Ostatni Zajazd na Litwie. historia Szlachecka z Roku 1811 i 1812 we Dwunastu Księgach Wierszem Pisana*, Paryż: A. Jełowicki.

Mickiewicz, Adam (1914), *Les Slaves: Cours Professé au Collège de France 1842-1844*, Paris: Musée Adam Mickiewicz.

Miłosz, Czesław (1969), *The History of Polish Literature*, London: Macmillan.

Olin, Margaret (2001), *The Nation Without Art: Examining Modern Discourses on Jewish Art*, Lincoln: University of Nebraska Press.

Ostrowski, Jan K. et al. (1999), *Land of the Winged Horsemen: Art in Poland (1572-1764)*, Alexandria: Art Services International.

Pelc, Janusz (2002), *Słowo i Obraz na Pograniczu Literatury i Sztuk Plastycznych*, Kraków: Universitas.

Poprzęcka, Maria (2000), *Arcydzieła Malarstwa Polskiego*, Warszawa: Arkady.

Sarbievius, Matthias Casimirus (1625), *Lyricorum Libri III*, Colonia Agrippina: s. n.

Van der Stock, Jan (1998), *Printing Images in Antwerp: The Introduction of Printmaking in a City (Fifteenth Century to 1585)*. Translated by Beverley Jackson, Rotterdam: Sound and Vision Interactive.

Van Haeften, Benedictus (1635), *Sacra Via Crucis*, Antwerp: s. n..

Vasmer, Max (1987), *Ètimologičeskij Slovar' Russkogo Jazyka*, Vol. 3, Moskva: Progress.

Walas, Teresa (2003), *Zrozumieć Swój Czas*, Kraków: Wydawnictwo Literackie.

Witkiewicz, Stanisław (1885), "Mickiewicz jako kolorysta." In: *Wędrowiec*, 49-53.

Zamoyski, Adam (1999), "History of Poland in the 16th-18th Centuries." In: Jan K. Ostrowski et al. *Land of the Winged Horsemen: Art in Poland (1572-1764)*. Alexandria: Art Services International.

Endnotes

1. "A native of Wilno, born into a Jewish family, Julian Klaczko wrote in Hebrew as a growing boy and was connected with the Jewish 'Haskalah' movement, but soon switched to Polish. After finishing his university studies in Germany (where he published in German), he moved to Paris and there won fame for his publicism, written in excellent French, which exerted considerable influence on public opinion" (see Miłosz 1969, pp. 260–261).

2. Vasmer (1987, pp. 665-667) notes two commonly heard etymological interpretations of the ethnonym *Słowianie* that are rejected nowadays on linguistic (i.e. morphological) grounds: 1) from the stem *sława* [glory] and 2) from the stem *słowo* [word]. According to Vasmer, the stem *Słow* most likely refers to a hydronym. Another Slavic linguist, Aleksander Brückner (1998, p. 501) interestingly links the ethnonym *Słowianie* to the gothic stem *slavan* [to be silent], which actually turns Klaczko's etymological explanation upside down.

3. See, for instance, Ostrowski et al. (1999) and Poprzęcka (2000). The present article partly draws on these historical surveys of Polish art.

4. The major texts in the nineteenth-century debate on the *raison-d'être* of Polish art have been collected in Klaczko (1961).

5. One could refer, for instance, to the well-known Belgian Polonist Backvis (1975, p. 757), who stated the following in one of his valuable studies on Polish Renaissance and Baroque literature: "Wiersze polskie, a nie płótna, należy przytaczać, aby znaleźć w tym kraju odpowiednik tego, co na Zachodzie znalazło wyraz w innowacjach Tintoretta, Velasqueza czy Rubensa!" ["We have to take into account Polish poems, not paintings, in order to find in this country the equivalent of what in the West found its expression in the innovating paintings of Tintoretto, Velasquez and Rubens!]" Another highly significant example of this visual sensitivity is the work of the already mentioned Polish "national poet" Adam Mickiewicz. Mickiewicz's writings have often been compared with paintings, and the poet himself has been called a true "colorist"—for instance, in the well-known essay "Mickiewicz jako kolorysta" (Mickiewicz as a Colorist) written by the Polish art critic Stanisław Witkiewicz (1885). Significant examples of this high level of "literary visuality" can also be found in the works of contemporary Polish poets, such as Julian Przyboś and Czesław Miłosz.

6. The original illustrations were made by Cornelis Galle; their Polish version was made by an anonymous Polish engraver.

7. Sarbiewski's *Lyricorum Libri* (*Books of Lyrics*, 1625) had some sixty editions in various countries of Europe, which—according to the Polish literary historian Miłosz (1969, p. 119)—allows us to say that "up to today no Polish poet has earned such fame abroad as did Sarbiewski in his lifetime and in the decades immediately following his death."

Verbal Above Visual: A Chinese Perspective

Ding Ning

There are a number of reasons why education in China has been predominantly verbal, and there is a great deal of evidence that can be used to argue that the visual has been effectively marginalized. In this essay, I will very briefly allude to two sources of the emphasis on the verbal—Imperial Examinations and the study of classics—and then turn to the study of art in contemporary Chinese universities.

1

In China, there is a very long and influential tradition called the *keju* [Imperial Examination], originally a method of selecting government officials. It was established in the Sui Dynasty (581–618) and lasted more than thirteen hundred years until the end of the Qing Dynasty (1644–1911). *Keju* was a wholly text-dominated examination (see, e.g., Yu 1932; Miyazaki 1976; Lee 1985; Chaffee 1995; Elman 2000).

The *xiangshi* [provincial examination] and the *huishi* [national examination] both required examinees have a firm grasp of the classical texts—for example, of Confucianism. There were a number of configurations of the test. In the *koushi*, or oral test, there were questions concerning the classics; for the mode called *tiejing*, parts of a chosen classical text were taught, and examinees were asked to fill in the missing lines or characters; in *moyi* [a simple written test], examinees were expected to answer questions concerning classical texts. Such questions could be relatively easy if the students were familiar with certain names, figures, and contexts relating to the texts in question. In answering questions in the *moyi*, no explanations were required. In the mode called *shifu*, on the other hand, students were required to compose poems or write rhymed and elaborated prose in accord with classical criteria. The successful candidates in the *shifu* were those with a sound knowledge of the rules and forms of classical poetry and prose.[1]

In part because of this long-standing examination system, the verbal plays a unique and paramount role in contemporary Chinese education; it seems that the *keju* still haunts the educational process. For example, the *gaokao* [National College and University Entrance Examination] has little to do with visual competence. In the Chinese-language portion of the examination, judges will ignore any illustrations in the test paper, even if they are pertinent to the argument. I imagine that illustrations would be regarded as a sort of distraction, and they might even reduce the student's score because grading the tests would be time consuming and mess up the test papers.

Candidates who want to be painters or sculptors would normally try to get into the academies of visual arts. Even so, they are then required do fairly well on the relevant language test—though their scores would be significantly lower than those required for university or college admission. There is little sign that this situation will change. Since 2000 increasing numbers of students have been enrolling at visual art academies but that has not meant the government or the interested public has paid any particular attention to visual competence.

2

Concerning painting in particular, I can offer three relevant conceptions of the verbal and the visual. First, brush-and-ink painting, as sort of the essence of classical Chinese art, is regarded as a form of writing. This is not only because so many painters, such as the late Song Dynasty's literati painters (Su Dongpo, Wen Tong, Mi Fu, Mi Youren, Wang Shen, Li Gonglin, Zhao Lingrang, Chao Buzhi, Li Shinan, and Huang Luzhi), were at the same time poets or writers but also because they were all trained as calligraphers before they painted anything with brush and ink. The techniques and the brushes are the same for painting and calligraphy. Zhang Yanyuan demonstrated this with his figure paintings, Kuo Xi with landscape, and Zhao Mengfu with paintings of flowers, bamboo, and rocks. In his inscription for the painting *Old Tree, Bamboo, Brambles, and Rock* [*xiushi sulin tu*], Zhao wrote, "rocks look like *feibai* [a style of cursive calligraphy characterized by hollow strokes, as if done with a half-dry brush]," and he added that "wood looks like Zhou style calligraphy." Zhao also compares what he calls the "writing" of bamboo with the eight strokes of the brush that are required to write the character (in this case, the word) *yong*: "writing bamboo one has to be familiar with the eight strokes of the character *yong*."[2] In other words, there is no difference between calligraphy and painting, but the former is the precondition of the latter.

Second, colophons (inscriptions) were more often taken as part of the composition of paintings and were understood to enhance the paintings' historical significance and aesthetic value. Inscriptions are often more than just poems or quotations—they were complex webs of allusions and quotations, intended to convey a poetic sentiment. Here, a commonly repeated anecdote is quite illuminating. In the enrollment examination at the Song Dynasty

Painting Academy, the question was, How can you paint "horse's hoofs becoming redolent after treading flowers"? (see Hu et al., 1982, p. 62). Very few examinees could think of a pictorial solution, but one talented student created a very suggestive painting in which some butterflies were depicted chasing a horse! It seems that if the painter does not have a deep knowledge and understanding of poetry, there can be no good painting at all.

Third, the importance of *writing* a painting is demonstrated by the unique concept of colors and the taste it requires to select them. It is a common trope in literati painting that ink contains *wuse* [five colors]. In practice, that meant black could vary and represent almost any color. If a painter used too many other colors, the painting might be considered vulgar. (see, e.g., Yu 1988). Sometimes pure (black) ink painting was taken to be the most elegant option. Here, the key role played by ink suggests the importance of writing with the brush.

3

From a very early stage, Chinese educational programs paid little attention to visual subjects. Basically, education during both the Shang and Zhou Dynasties was for the ruling class: In the Shang Dynasty, subjects of study included *jisi* [sacrifice], military affairs, music and dance, and literacy; in the Zhou Dynasty, education also encompassed *liuyi* [the six arts]. The six arts were *li* [the ancient code of behavior and the norm for the maintenance of patriarchy and hierarchy], music, shooting, *yu* [martial arts], calligraphy, and arithmetic. It was believed that "music cultivates the mind" along with *li* [manners] (see Anon 1999, p. 634). Both *li* and music acted as means of refining one's personality and becoming a responsive and responsible member of society.[3]

Many influential Chinese thinkers emphasized time and again the role of *li*, which meant, in a general sense, moral education. This is given voice in a collection of texts called *lunyu* [*Analects*], containing sayings and dialogues attributed to Confucius (551–479 BCE; the text was compiled by his disciples after his death).[4] In some sense, the more Confucius stressed *li*, the more likely that sensibility was neglected. For example, one text enjoins the reader "to look at nothing in defiance of *li*, to listen to nothing in defiance of *li*, to speak of nothing in defiance of *li*, and never to stir hand or foot in defiance of *li*."[5] Although Confucius thought both moral education and what might be called knowledge education were essential, the latter was always pivotal. He nominated the *Six Classics*—known in Chinese as the *shi, shangshu, li, yue, yi*, and *chunqiu*—as the principal textbooks for all education (see Mao et al., 1979, p. 47). Five of the six are wholly without illustrations or thematic engagement with the visual.[6]

Yi, fifth of the *Six Classics*, the *Book of Changes* or *I Ching*, conveys the view of the universe, ethnics, and dialectics (Lynn 1994).[7] Here, it may seem that the text is at last visual because of the preeminence of trigrams and other schemata. Rudolf Arnheim has written a fascinating article on the *taiji* emblem in the book, which symbolizes the yin-and-yang principle. The word *taiji* literally means the "great map of the poles." Arnheim describes the "map's" signification:

> The visual design and the essence of the thoughts for which the figure stands are simple enough to make a concrete and fairly complete analysis possible; they are, on the other hand, sufficiently rich and subtle to be acceptable as an example of the kind of symbolism psychiatrists, anthropologists, and philosophers are concerned with (see Arnheim 1966).

The *taiji* emblem is abstract; otherwise, it would be too specific and not as rich in philosophical significance. And yet this and the centuries of controversy regarding the *I Ching* are not primarily visual: visual literacy has little to do with the book despite its famous trigrams.

Despite centuries of ongoing secondary scholarship on the classics, it remains the case that their uses and reception are resolutely nonvisual (see Anon 1999). Confucius believed in reflection guided by the classics, and he wrote that "one who learns but does not think is lost. One who thinks but does not learn is in great danger" (Lun 1999, p. 15). That doctrine, at its foundation, is not visual primarily because it is ethically oriented. Considering the reception histories of the texts, and following the lead of their mainly ethical purposes, it would be possible to construct an argument that the verbal has played the preeminent role in education—and that remains true today.[8]

4

I will conclude with some remarks on the current situation in Chinese universities. I concentrate on them, instead of art academies, because in the nature of things there are far more students enrolled in universities. I begin with some qualitative observations on visual competence in college-level (third level) education.

Although art education in Chinese universities and colleges has been strengthened significantly since the later 1970s, following the so-called Cultural Revolution, there is currently a strong interest in the establishment of "arts teaching sections," which are not solely for students who major in various fields of the arts but for students who are studying in any field. It is a trend that significantly dilutes whatever visual education such students might otherwise receive. In the major comprehensive universities, undergraduates, regardless of their subjects of study, are required to have at least two credits in the arts before their graduation. That means every undergraduate student should attend at least one art education course. Yet, as far as I know, the available courses—such as Chinese art history, Chinese art and craft, Western art history, the history of architecture, and the study of visual stories in the Bible—comprise only a small part of the sum total of art education courses. A large percentage of students choose courses in music (even popular music), movies, drama, and dance. Sometimes they pick dubious courses as well—for example, aesthetics and philosophy of art, a subject that is likely to involve only a little consideration of artworks because most tutors in the subject have trained in departments of philosophy or Chinese language and literature. In my experience, the tutors' experience and knowledge of the arts is at times questionable. Students in the aesthetics and philosophy of art will learn some big names—such as Kant, Hegel, Heidegger, Derrida, Goodman, and Arnheim— but few will read their texts or study the relevant works of art.

Surely, to be visually literate, students must enroll in courses on visual art. As a matter of fact, a lot of students attend no courses of the kind, and it is no wonder that some of them are almost totally ignorant of art history. Once I guided a group of students in Paris; none of them had visited France. One student from the business school hesitated to enter the Louvre because she did not think that it was wise to go into the museum while it was so sunny outside. She had no passion for painting and sculpture, let alone for visual literacy. There is, I would say, quite a quite long way to go before most Chinese university or college students could be considered to be visually literate.

5

The situation at the graduate level (MA or PhD) is different. Students who study art history, for instance, would have learned both Chinese and Western art history before they enroll at the graduate level. Usually there are three kinds of students: those who concentrate on art theory, those who study Chinese art history, and those who specialize in foreign art history. In a rough count, there are about twenty institutions in China that offer graduate programs in these subjects.[9]

Students of art theory have to study a number of difficult texts, including the many volumes of *zhongguo gudai hualun* [ancient Chinese painting theory], of which only a few bear substantial relations to extant works.[10] That is why some graduate theses and dissertations have elaborated on such subjects as *qi* (in this instance to be translated as "breathing"), without going into the details of any particular painting. I have also seen a PhD dissertation on Nietzsche's thoughts on Greek art, which had no reference to any artworks. Inevitably, in inquiries like these, some out-of-date conclusions, like that of Winckelmann's impression of Greek art, have been blindly quoted.

For students who study "foreign art history" the situation is analogous. Because most students in China do not have a chance to go abroad before writing their dissertations, they have to rely on reference books. The more foreign languages a student reads, the more he or she comprehends differing points of view and assesses history from a wider horizon—but the learning is basically text oriented. The basic reference works are usually books (articles and offprints are significantly more rare). Here is a list of general reference works for art history students at Peking University, compiled in spring 2005:

> *Art across Time* (Adams 2002), *Key Monuments of the Baroque* (Adams 2000), *Key Monuments of the Italian Renaissance* (Adams 2000), *Italian Renaissance Art* (Adams 2001), and *A History of Western Art* (Adams 2001); *Word and Image: French Painting of the Ancient Régime* (Bryson 1981); *Poussin's Paintings* (Carrier 1993); *The Oxford Dictionary of Art* (Chilvers et al., 1988); *Culture and Value* (Cunningham and Reich 1982); *Stories of Art* (Elkins 2002); *The Story of Art* (Gombrich 1978); *Illustrated Dictionary of Symbols in Eastern and Western Art* (Hall and Puleston 1996); *History of Art* (Jason 1991); *The Oxford History of Western Art* (Kemp 2000); *Gardner's Art Through the Ages* (Kleiner and Mamiya 2005); *The Gallery Companion: Understanding Western Art* (Lodwick 2002); *The Faber Book of Art Anecdotes* (Lucie-Smith 1992); *What Great Paintings Say* (Hagen 1995); *The Renaissance: Studies in Art and Poetry* (Pater 1986); and *Art: A Brief History* (Stokstad 2000).

For students who specialize in Greek art, the list is about four times as long and includes more specialized monographs along with popular works.[11]

Surprisingly, students of Chinese art history are even more verbally directed. It is difficult for students in the mainland China to view original works, particularly older paintings, because many are in the Palace Museum in Taipei. Students are compelled to make full use of the available texts—a limitation that may not be seen as such because of the dependence of literati painting on often subtle and sophisticated inscriptions and seals. To identify and understand the colophons and seals, most of which quote classical poetry, students have to build a solid foundation in ancient Chinese language, classical literature, material culture, philosophy, and history. That kind of knowledge is not exactly iconographical because the tie between the image and the inscription can be indirect in various ways.[12]

Certainly it is essential for students to read a large number of texts, and I am not saying that images, even those encountered only in reproductions, are not just as important for students to grasp. On the contrary, the verbal materials are included in the curriculum for the purpose of illuminating the rich connotations of the images—not vice versa. The interpretation of images should be the primary and uppermost task of art history. It would not be right to discard the verbal in the field of Chinese art history for the sake of focusing on images, but at the same time—and even though it goes against the tenor of centuries of Chinese cultural awareness—the indulgence in texts should be avoided or even ended.

References

Adams, Laurie Schneider (2000), *Key Monuments of the Baroque*, Boulder: Westview Press.

Adams, Laurie Schneider (2000), *Key monuments of the Italian Renaissance*, Boulder and Oxford; Westview Press.

Adams, Laurie Schneider (2001), *Italian Renaissance Art*, Boulder: Westview Press.

Adams, Laurie Schneider (2002), *Art across Time*, Boston, McGraw-Hill.

Adams, Laurie Schneider (2008), *A History of Western Art*, Boston: McGraw-Hill.

Anon (1999) "Book of Rites." In: *Notes and Commentaries on Thirteen Classics*, Beijing: Peking University Press.

Arnheim, Rudolf (1966), "Analysis of a Symbol of Interaction." In: *Toward a Psychology of Art: Collected Essays*, Berkeley: University of California Press.

Beazley, John Davidson (1986), *Development of the Attic Black-Figure, Revised edition*, Berkeley: University of California Press.

Bryson, Norman (1981), *Word and Image: French Painting of the Ancient Régime*, Cambridge: Cambridge University Press.

Carrier, David (1993), *Poussin's Paintings: A Study in Art-Historical Methodology*, University Park, Pennsylvania State University Press.

Cao Xueqin (1973), *The Story of the Stone*. Translated from Chinese by David Hawkes, 5 Vol. (1973–1986), London: Penguin.

Chaffee, John (1995), *The Thorny Gates of Learning in Sung China: A Social History of Examinations*, Albany: State University of New York Press.

Chilvers, Ian, Osborne, Harold & Farr, Dennis (1988), *The Oxford Dictionary of Art*, Oxford and New York: Oxford University Press.

Clark, Andrew, Elston, Maya & Hart, Mary Louise (2002), *Understanding Greek Vases: A Guide to Terms, Styles, and Techniques*, Los Angeles: J. Paul Getty Museum.

Cook, B. F. (1998), *Reading the Past: Greek Inscriptions*, Berkeley and Los Angeles: University of California Press.

Cunningham, Lawrence S. & Reich, John J. (1982), *Culture and Values*, 2 Vol., New York: Holt, Rinehart and Winston.

Dobson, W. A. C. H. (1968), *The Language of the Book of Songs*, Toronto: University of Toronto Press.

Elkins, James (2002), *Stories of Art*, New York: Routledge.

Elman, Benjamin (2000), *A Cultural History of Civil Examinations in Late Imperial China*, Berkeley: University of California Press.

Gombrich, E. H. (1978), *The Story of Art*, Oxford: Phaidon.

Hacker, Edward, Moore, Steve, & Patsco, Lorraine eds. (2002), *I Ching: An Annotated Bibliography*, New York: Routledge.

Hagen, Rose-Marie & Hagen, Rainer (1995), *What Great Paintings Say*, 3 Vol. (1995–1997), Köln and New York: Taschen.

Hall, James & Puleston, Chris (1996), *Illustrated Dictionary of Symbols in Eastern and Western Art*, New York: IconEditions.

Hollander, Anne (1993), *Seeing Through Clothes*, Berkeley: University of California Press.

Hu Zhenlang et al. eds. (1982), *Stories of Chinese Painting*, Shanghai: Shanghai People's Art Publishing House.

Janson, Horst Woldemar (1991), *History of Art*, New York: Harry N. Abrams.

Kemp, Martin, ed. (2000), *The Oxford History of Western Art*, Oxford and New York: Oxford University Press.

Kleiner, Fred S., & Mamiya, Christin (2005), *Gardner's Art Through the Ages: The Western Perspective*, Belmont: Wadsworth.

Knoblock, John & Riegel, Jeffrey (2000), *The Annals of Lü Buwei: A Complete Translation and Study*. Translated from Chinese by John Knobloch and Jeffrey Riegel, Stanford: Stanford University Press.

Lodwick, Marcus (2002), *The Gallery Companion: Understanding Western Art*, London: Thames & Hudson.

Lee, Thomas (1985), *Government Education and Examinations in Sung China*, New York: St. Martin's.

Lucie-Smith, Edward ed. (1992), *The Faber Book of Art Anecdotes*, London: Faber and Faber.

Lun Yu (1999), *The Analects*, Book II. Translated from Chinese by Arthur Waley and Yang Bojun, Changsha: Hunan People's Publishing House and Beijing: Foreign Language Press.

Lynn, Richard (1994), *The Classic of Changes: A New Translation of the "I Ching" as Interpreted by Wang Bi*. Translated by Richard Lynn, New York: Columbia University Press.

Mao Lirui et al. eds. (1979), *History of Ancient Chinese Education*, Beijing: People's Education Publishing House.

Miyazaki Ichisada (1976), *China's Examination Hell: The Civil Service Examinations of Imperial China*. Translated from Chinese by Conrad Schirokauer, New York: Weatherhill.

Pater, Walter (1986), *The Renaissance: Studies in Art and Poetry*, Oxford and New York: Oxford University Press.

Pandermalis, Dimitrios (2004), *Alexander the Great: Treasures from an Epic Era of Hellenism*, New York: Alexander S. Onassis Public Benefit Foundation.

Pollitt, J. J. (1974), *The Ancient View of Greek Art: Criticism, History, and Terminology*, New Haven and London: Yale University Press.

Richter, Gisela M. A. (1987), *A Handbook of Greek Art: A Survey of the Visual Arts of Ancient Greece*, New York Da Capo Press.

Shandong Pictorial Press (1996), *Lao Zhaopian*, Shangdong: Shandong Pictorial Press.

Stokstad, Marilyn (2000), *Art: A Brief History*, New York: Harry N. Abrams.

Van Norden, Bryan ed. (2002), *Confucius and the Analects: New Essays,* New York: Oxford University Press.

Yu Feian, (1988) *Chinese Painting Colors: Studies of Their Preparation and Application in Traditional and Modern Times.* Translated from Chinese by Jerome Silbergeld and Amy McNair, Hong Kong: Hong Kong University Press.

Yu Jianhua ed. (1998), *Classified Edition of Ancient Chinese Painting Criticism*, 2 Vol., Beijing: People's Fine Art Publishing House.

Yu Yuan Chang (1934), "Civil Service Examination System in China, 1644-1905," PhD dissertation, unpublished, Columbia University.

Zhao Mengfu (n.d.), *Old Tree, Bamboo, Brambles, and Rock.* [Painting]. Palace Museum, Beijing.

Endnotes

1. English speakers can get an idea of the difficulties involved by reading the descriptions in Cao (1973), in which the characters play at examination-style poetry games. –J.E.]

2. See Zhao's (n.d.) inscription in his *Old Tree, Bamboo, Brambles, and Rock* (*xiushi sulin tu*).

3. The value accorded them is partly because both *li* and music could also be incorporated into other activities—for instance, shooting arrows has something to do with both subjects, because all actions should conform to rules of *li*, and the rhythm of actions agrees with that of music.

4. For *li* see further Van Norden (2002).

5. That passage also explains why Confucius never talked about matters that were strange, overwhelming, chaotic, and spectral. Confucius, *Analects,* Book XII, *yanyuan*; translation by the author.

6. *Shi* (the *Classic of Poetry*, or *Book of Songs*) is China's earliest poetry anthology, collected and edited around the mid-sixth century BCE. The 305 songs fall into three parts: *feng* (wind), which is mostly folk songs; *ya* (elegance), composed of songs sung at official banquets; and *song* (odes), songs chanted at sacrificial ceremonies of the nobility (for a study of these and other terms see Dobson (1968)]. *Shangshu* (the *Noble Book*), second of the *Six Classics*, is one of the central works of Confucianism. *Li*, third of the *Six Classics*, refers to the *Book of Rites*, which was partly compiled by Confucius himself. It was for teaching good manners and the emphasis was on the inner world, which was to be cultivated following the requirements set up by Confucianism. *Yue,* fourth of the *Six Classics*, the *Classics of Music*, is unfortunately lost. However, it is believed that this textbook was also intended for *li* education as well, because music was thought to help build a sense of harmony, and the ideal combination of both *li* and music was just what Confucius expected. *Chunqiu* (the *Spring and Autumn Annals*), last of the *Six Classics*, is a history book. Written chronologically, it records the history of the period between 777 and 481 BCE; it was said that the book was edited by Confucius himself and that Lu, the place that is chronicled in the book, was actually his homeland (see Knobloch and Riegel 2000).

7. A good place to start with the *I Ching* is Hacker et al., (2002).

8. One might notice that contemporary Chinese publishers now pay a great deal of attention to books with illustrations because they believe we are now in an era of reading pictures. Such an opinion has little to do with visual literacy; many books of the kind serve certain nostalgic sentiments and do not include discussion of theoretical issues concerning visual literacy. (An example in China is *Old Photographs* (*lao zhaopian*; 1996); it is essentially what would be called coffee-table publishing, now more than 12 volumes available.

9. The main Chinese institutions which offer MA and/or PhD degrees in art history and theory are as follows: Peking University, Tsinghua University, Capital Normal University, Central Academy of Fine Arts, China Academy of Arts, China National Academy of Fine Arts, Southeastern University, Shanghai University, Xi'an Academy of Fine Arts, Nanjing Arts School, Nanjing Normal University, Sichuan University, Sichuan Academy of Fine Arts, Luxun Academy of Fine Arts, Guangzhou Academy of Fine Arts, Zhongshan University, Shangdong Arts School, and the Hubei Academy of Fine Arts.

10. The most influential anthology is edited by Yu (1998).

11. For example, Beazley (1986), Clark, et al., (2002), Cook (1998), Pollitt (1974), and Richter (1987) as well as more popular titles such as Hollander (1993) or Pandermalis (2004).

12. [This emphasis on textual analysis of colophons and seals has a long and contested history in the Western scholarship of Chinese painting. It has been critiqued for several decades, for example, by James Cahill; and in general, expertise in reading colophons remains the province of scholars trained in China. A dossier on this subject is forthcoming from Jason Kuo at the University of Maryland; he is preparing a book of interviews with several dozen historians of Chinese art. –J.E.]

To Read, To Look: Teaching Visual Studies in Moscow

Viktoria Musvik

In *Art and Illusion* (1960) Ernst Gombrich describes several examples of drawings from various epochs—including buildings, cities, and animals. Among the animal pictures is a thirteenth-century drawing of a lion by Villiard de Honnecourt that was done in the presence of a real lion but looks like a heraldic or ornamental image; a nineteenth-century engraving of the cathedral of Notre Dame in Chartres that efficiently erases Romanesque windows of the building; a sixteenth-century woodcut of the locusts that invaded Europe—supposedly the "exact counterfeit" even though they look more like horses; and an eighteenth-century image of a rhinoceros that is said to be the first pictures of a rhinoceros done without "preconceived prejudices and inattention"—even though it repeats the prejudices of Albrecht Dürer's famous woodcut.

Drawing on these and some other examples, Gombrich argues that here we are dealing with the psychology of vision. According to him, every artistic rendering of reality, especially the new and the unknown, will necessarily start from a handy cliché or stereotype that will then be adjusted "through trial and error." It is interesting, therefore, to see how many visual observations are "allowed to enter into the formula." There is no such thing as a "faithful record of visual experience," only "a faithful construction of a relational model." Gombrich comes to the conclusion that this is not due to the subjectivity of vision but to its richness and the "complexity of information that reaches us"; he concludes that "those who understand the notation derive no false information" from such images (see Gombrich 1989).

Even so, that last phrase brings with it ambiguity and the notion of "visual literacy" or "visual competence." The question is how well and to what extent a person looking at an artificially constructed image (whether it is drawn, painted, designed, or otherwise built) can understand the conventionality of what she sees. It can seem a more or less idle problem provided we are speaking about drawings of lions and locusts, but it becomes increasingly important in cultures that seem to build their political or ideological notion of the minimal level of visual literacy—and indeed their whole identity—on two paradoxical points: the claim that their society is "predominantly verbal" (and so there seems to be no special need to either study or produce images) and the actual practice of visually rich communal rituals that are one of the main factors that maintain and support political power.

This is especially true in the case of Russia. Since at least the times of Ivan the Terrible, Russian culture has been based on a paradoxical (not to say potentially and practically dangerous) relationship between the glamorous—even opulent—visual representation of the concept of power and the active discouragement of any form of visual literacy— whether it is a critical reflection on one's first-hand visual experience or the attention to the details of images that were meant for meditation, admiration, or idolatry.

The vacillation between the idea that Russian culture is a predominantly verbal one and the idea that its own attitude to visuality is radically different from the overly garish Western tradition is a recurrent topos in Russia's philosophy and theology.[1] The contemporary argument is very similar to the one that is described in this book by Kris van Heuckelom (see Chapter 4), and because I would like concentrate on a different aspect of the problem of "cultural mediation on the physiological process of seeing," I will not go into detail on this point. It is enough to say that the idea that Russian culture is mostly verbally oriented is still a living force, a recurrent topic, even among artistic bohemians and intellectuals.

Here, in place of the longer argument, is an example. In my recent interview with Vladimir Fridkes, one of the leading Russian contemporary artists and fashion photographers (he is also one of the members of the art quartet AES+F), Fridkes remarked:

We call our work "digital painting." And some Russian critics have accused it of "spectacularity," meaning that visuality prevails over ideas. It's, sort of, "too beautiful". . . What is Russian culture? It is theater, word, poetry, literature. And where is the visual? There is no visual. The Russian school of painting is fairly derivative. Even the Kremlin was built by Italians. I wouldn't like to belittle or berate anyone, but any Russian would say that this culture is mainly theater, together with the great Russian literature and poetry— but never that the culture includes great Russian painting. A Westerner, on the other hand, is raised on painting and architecture. For a Westerner, the word "spectacular" isn't a curse. They look and say "Wow, this is beautiful!" and they are happy. A Russian looks and says "No, this is too beautiful." We are used to the idea that conceptualism is our main force (Musvik 2008).

I find this quotation immensely revealing. It is true that an average Western person sees more art, especially contemporary art, in his or her life and knows more about it than an average Russian person. But it is also true that the words "visual" or "spectacular" often do not pertain to art at all. Yet, it seems that for Fridkes the sphere of the "spectacular" [*spektakul'arnii*] or the "visual" is not connected in any way to theater or spectacle. The idea that the visual denotes just painting or photography—that is, it denotes art as opposed to more mundane and less sacred spheres of human life—seems to be a recurring one in Russia, and not only among artists. Paradoxically enough, Fridkes is also, as he himself points out, happy to do both practical visual things and contemporary art. What's more, *Action Half Life* (2003-2005)[2] , the project that he is describing in the excerpt I have quoted, is actually a parody that the group AES+F created, making fun of the world of glamour, glossy magazines, artificiality, and the pervasive simulacrum. In a way, *Action Half Life* is conceptual art that tries to reflect on the concept of visual and at the same time to use the idea of beauty to make conceptual art beautiful. *Action Half Life* tries, in a very intellectual and self-reflective way, to marry the two concepts. And yet Fridkes excludes the concept of spectacle—the idea that is closest to what he is doing—from the field of the visual and equates it with the verbal.

If I had asked him to clarify this point, I think Fridkes would have happily erased the word *theater* from his list of nonvisual fields of culture ("theater, word, poetry, literature") and elaborated instead on the concept of simulacrum. His claim, in that sense, was one of those slips of the tongue that are supposedly without symptomatic meaning. Or, he might have said that he meant theater as a genre, not as spectacle—that he understood theater as something rooted in the activity of playwrights. But I find his actual words indicative of a certain discontinuity between theory and practice, between "free" ideas and oppressive communal habits, between the power of reason and desire—what I understand as a dangerous paradox inherent in Russian culture. In the long run, it comes to the problem of the "inattentive observer,"[3] who lives in a culture that is deeply ritualized and theatrical, a society that uses the idea of the visual in a tremendously complex way that goes far beyond the concept of art as high art—and yet is unable to reflect on his own practices of vision because he is not taught to do so (or better, he is actually actively discouraged from any such analysis). The result is a person who either sees too little in the visual elements of culture or, if he or she is learned and socially active, reads too much into images but never sees enough.[4] Such a person is unable to go sufficiently beyond a criticism of the regime (and sometimes such protest takes extreme and even shocking forms, as the work of AES+F shows) to find practical, everyday, individual ways of dealing with this spectacular, visually striking and even overwhelming culture that constantly proclaims itself to be nonvisual.

In a way, one feels that the idea that Russian culture is more verbal than visual and is far behind Europe in its use of the "spectacular," whether it is a matter of contemporary art, advertising or, for example, elaborate Renaissance festivals, is very useful when it comes to politics, power, and manipulation. One is constantly taught either to overlook the role of the visual in Russia or, when it comes to reflection, to reproduce (or, to put it cynically, simulate) the Western discourse of contemporary art or the humanities—especially when it comes to problems that are not paramount for our society. The issues that *are* supreme for us, including the specific role of the visual, are covered by a thick layer of alien problems and assumptions, a screen that makes our own past and present opaque. Recently, we have witnessed several new projects that illustrated this thesis: the Moscow Biennale of Contemporary Art, inaugurated in 2005, and the Kandinsky Prize. The latter was big, picturesque, and totally void of "real life issues" though it claimed the opposite, as was noted by many Russia's influential contemporary art critics (see Kandinsky Prize 2007)[5].

The problem I am describing is sometimes discussed in studies of Soviet ideology, but it very rarely (if ever) goes beyond that. This essay is not an overall study of this tendency, rather it is an attempt to show, using a couple of isolated examples from different historical epochs, that the problem of the "inattentive observer" is neither a contemporary Russian issue nor a specifically Soviet one but that it has far deeper roots and has in fact been repeated for several centuries without much variation.

1

My first example dates back to the beginning of the seventeenth century.[6] In November 1600, the Russian ambassador to England Grigorii Mikulin noted this in his diary:

> On the seventeenth day of November they [the Ambassador's retinue] were visited by the Queen's nobleman, Lord Windsor who, taking off his hat, conveyed to Grigorii the queen's words: "Our Queen Elizabeth has ordered you to be present tonight after the dinner…"
>
> And Grigorii and Ivashko, taking off their hats, answered: "Praised be the God and the Queen; we will do as the queen wishes."
>
> On the same day Grigorii and Ivashko went to the Queen. And when they came to her chamber, the Queen inquired after their health and said to Grigorii: "This time today I am celebrating the day when I acceded to the throne; and because of that I ordered you to be present here and see my entertainment." And she told Grigorii and Ivashko to stand in her chamber and to watch the entertainment.
>
> And Grigorii and Ivashko saw the Queen's entertainment: how in her presence princes and lesser nobles fought with lances, and the noblemen were in full armour and mounted on the mares and stallions; and at this time the only other ambassadors or envoys at the Queen's court were the King of Barbary's emissaries, and they stood in the yard under the shed with the common people. [Besstuzhev-Riumin 1893]

In this entry from the ambassadorial report [*stateinyi spisok*], Mikulin describes one of the most magnificent of Elizabethan court celebrations, the Accession Day tournament. Mikulin's visit to England lasted about eight months. He and his subordinate, the diplomatic official [*pod'iachii*] Ivan Zinov'ev left Moscow in May 1600, arrived in England on 14 September 1600, and left on 23 May 1601. The event Mikulin describes took place on 17 November.

Stateinyi spisok was the type of official report used in Russian recordkeeping from the late fifteenth century to the beginning of the eighteenth century and was part of an elaborate system of diplomatic documentation.[7] The 1600 report includes the description of four main Elizabethan court celebrations: the royal entry into London on 5 November; the Accession Day celebration on 17 November; the celebration of Epiphany or the Twelfth Day; and the celebration of St. George's Day on 23 April, along with the descriptions of other events, most notably a detailed description of Essex's revolt and even a few words about the royal hunt. The descriptions of court celebrations are of different lengths, which clearly indicate the author's attitude toward them. It is perhaps no wonder that the longest and the most detailed description is dedicated to the celebration of Epiphany, which was one of the main state holidays in Russia. It is strange, however, that the description of the Accession Day celebrations, which were one of the main and most solemn state celebrations in Elizabethan times, is the shortest of the four and the least precise.

This is surprising, to say the least. We know that under Queen Elizabeth, the celebration of the day of her accession to the throne "was… developed as a major state festival with celebrations on a national scale" (Strong 1977, p. 114). At court from the beginning of the 1570s, the event was celebrated by a tournament and a carefully staged pageant. The participants were accompanied by their retainers, who were often dressed as allegorical personages, and there was a pageant wagon carrying musicians and actors. Those who could not understand the elaborate imagery would still have been impressed by the magnificent spectacle. Nevertheless, the Russian visitors were clearly *not* impressed. In the passage of the report quoted above, only a minimal amount of information is given about the tilt, for example, and the description of the whole celebration is different from the other three descriptions, both in form and in content.

Elsewhere I have analyzed this difference from three points of view: what is described (or omitted), how it is described, and why (Musvik 2002). I have suggested that in Mikulin's account when a celebration was of a known type, and was considered sufficiently important, it would be described by certain formulas. For instance, he described English court celebrations for which he could find direct parallels in Russian culture and in describing them he followed models he got from Russian chronicles; however, when the details or the event itself were unknown or seemed unimportant, the structure of the description was very different.

The Accession Day tournament was the most alien type of celebration of the four that Mikulin saw in England. The Western idea of a formal tournament, to say nothing of the elaborate and carefully prepared tournaments of late medieval and Renaissance Europe staged to honor the monarch, was unknown in Russia. There were fist and staff fights and judicial combats in Russia in the sixteenth century, but they were not included in the same category of celebrations as religious festivals. They could even be considered diabolical: in sixteenth- and seventeenth-century Russia, the Church mistrusted music and drama, and theater was forbidden until the middle of the seventeenth century (Gudzy 1970). Therefore, the whole idea of celebrating the Tsar with elaborate theatrical shows, tournaments, or dances would have seemed to the Russian courtiers outrageous and even blasphemous.[8] Thus, for the ambassador, the Queen's tournament was not experienced as part of an elaborate ritual and ceremonial connected with the assertion of sacred royal power.

The Russian ambassador does not seem to be keen on either trusting his eyes or noticing what he is shown. There is no sense of the "otherness" of the foreign culture. He does not try to explain or understand the unusual rituals or try to see the real place that this or that event has in the foreign culture. In other cases he simply "translates" what little he notices into his known system of values and images. There are many clichés in Mikulin's account, both linguistic and cultural—for example, the phrase about the presence of no other ambassadors (which signifies the importance of the Russian embassy) and the description of the invitation to the Queen are repeated, almost word by word, in many other diplomatic accounts of the period.

It is a well-known fact that the use of clichés in descriptions of the unknown, on the one hand, and the special interest in the etiquette, enumeration, and the matters of hierarchy, on the other hand, were part of a system of interpretation that persisted in Russian culture up to the end of the seventeenth century. It could be called conventional or normative. It existed in literature; in icon-painting, where the canon played the central role; in chronicle illustration; and in everyday life (see Musvik 2002, p. 237–240). The rigid order and hierarchy of the religious procession, the observance of the known ritual were in themselves sources of meaning. In the chronicles, for instance, the use of certain clichés confirmed the tradition and affirmed the historicity of the document, even though the descriptions were sometimes invented or falsified, because they showed not what happened but what should have happened (Likhachev 1947, 1970). On the other hand, the new and the unknown—and therefore the uncodified—were often seen as evil or anomalous. In early Russian travel literature, as Iurii Lotman and Boris Uspenskii have shown (Lotman 1992; Uspenskii 1994), all countries were clearly divided into good lands and bad lands. Voyages to foreign countries were compared to trips to sinful places, and Russian travelers who went to foreign lands were mourned over as dead.

What I find immensely revealing here for the question of visual literacy is the absence of attention to those magnificent visual elements of the Elizabethan court celebrations that would have required personal interpretation. It is pertinent that the complex symbolism of the Accession Day tournament was the most "unformulaic" type of English royal celebration. The Russian court celebrations of this epoch mostly relied on extra-personal elements, on the application of known, set formulas to the visible forms. They did not permit different readings. Elizabethan spectacles, by contrast, admitted both impersonal and personal interpretations; as every early modern historian knows, the latter could be rather ambiguous and open to various, often paradoxical or even opposite readings.

In the seventeenth century, the Russian system of formal etiquette codified the world and confirmed the tradition of which they were a part. Such etiquette was not peculiar to medieval Russian culture; the same attitude can be seen in medieval Western travel accounts. At the end of the sixteenth century and the beginning of the seventeenth century, the methodology of geographical and historical research and the ways of interpreting other cultures were rapidly changing in the West (Hodgen 1964). What is significant here is that in Russia, those changes took place only in the eighteenth century—and even then, the "inattentive observer" has not altogether disappeared. Rather, he has survived all modernizations and "Westernizations." We encounter him (or her, for that matter) again in the Soviet epoch.

2

Much has been written on the various aspects of Soviet spectacles and rituals; however, in my opinion, the most revealing example of the "inattentive observer" is given in Mikhail Allenov (2003)'s article "The Visibility of Systemic Absurdity in the Moscow Metro's Emblematics." In his paper, Allenov poses a very straightforward question that is almost frightening in its simplicity: "How," he asks, "have these monstrous events [in our history], that seem absurd or impossible, became not only possible but real?" His first answer is in the form of another question; perhaps, he wonders, what now seems patently absurd, both culturally and visually (for example, in the Metro's architecture) was not understood as such. Yet his essay goes against this assumption, and he argues that the absurd was fully exposed to the public and yet somehow escaped everyone's attention.

Allenov limits himself to just one striking example: the Moscow underground station Komsomolskaia. Every year I take my visual studies students there to illustrate the notion of visual literacy. The station was designed by the famous Soviet architect Aleksei Shusev along with five of his colleagues (including the artist Pavel Korin) and opened on 30 January 1952, thirteen months before Stalin's death. This is perhaps one of the most (if not the most) magnificent stations in the Moscow Metro, and it is not surprising that Shusev and Korin received the Stalin prize. There are 68 marble columns; the length of the station is 190 meters (the standard length is about 160 meters), and the hall is huge— 12 meters wide and 9 meters long. The floor is covered with gray granite. The most visually interesting feature is the ceiling. It has eight mosaic panels, designed by Korin, set with smalt and precious stones. The subject of the panels is the Soviet victory in World War II and other triumphs of the Russian State, starting with Alexander Nevskii's victory over the Teutonic knights in the Battle of the Ice in 1242.

What matters for my argument is a nonnarrative segment of the ceiling—a false blue sky cupola. It is situated over the steps that lead to the passage from one metro line to another. In the center of this small blue dome is a five-rayed star with a magnificent chandelier pendent hanging from its center. Just in front, the star is a surreally strange and an unexpected object in a marble frame: a hatch that looks like it is covered in iron bars. Situated on the central axis of the overall sequence of ceiling panels, this strange design asks to be read as part of the narrative sequence, which would run something like this: victory–triumph–battle–victory–Lenin–victory–iron bars (!)–magnificent blue sky–triumphant star. As Allenov points out, the strange vision of prison bars (they are actually iron bars that hide a ventilation duct) is framed and included in the narrative, on equal terms with all the other images. According to Allenov, the absurdity of the sequence is evident—and so is the danger, fear, and cruelty of the system that does not even try to hide itself behind pompous images of victories and the happy life that should follow.

One of my students noticed another detail that makes the absurdity blatantly obvious. And yet it is easily overlooked. The main theme of sequence of panels is not just the idea of power, but the historical validation of the Stalinist regime. It would seem logical, therefore, that the sequence should be seen by the spectator in its historical order: first the Battle of the Ice and last the Soviet victory in World War II. In reality, however, it is impossible to make a continuous and uninterrupted narrative out of these eight isolated episodes, because they are turned on the ceiling in such a way that the historical narrative is reversed: time flows backward, from the victory in World War II back through earlier episodes to the Battle of the Ice.

Komsomolskaia is one of the busiest and most crowded stops, connecting three railway stations, and no one goes there for fun. The whole beautifully designed and executed ensemble of the station is, paradoxically, not addressed to the interested or watchful observer, not meant for detailed analysis. Such an observer is, one might say, actively discouraged: the sequence is effectively designed for the average, inattentive spectator who should be overwhelmed by the opulence of the colors, sizes, materials but who does not have enough time or will to go into the iconography in detail.

There is, however, one further question to ask. For my own students, the absurdity of this "reversed time sequence" was far more evident than Allenov's analysis of the "vision of the iron bars," which he wrote in 1980s and published only very recently. My students have asked me if Allenov might not be reading a bit too much into these iron bars. Allenov does identify some of the more obvious features of the station, but the "vision of the iron bars" dominates his witty and ironical essay. One can say, of course, that my students—born at the very beginning of Gorbachev's perestroika—just do not understand the feeling of fear that pervaded the 1980s and so fail to appreciate Allenov's wit and courage and his identification with the intelligentsia. We, who are only ten or fifteen years older, would never have asked such questions: we were too much in opposition to the then collapsing regime and too much in awe of our teachers. Yet, my students have already learned to trust their own minds and senses, especially their sense of vision—perhaps more than they trust the written word, and the constructions of "authorities" like Allenov.[9]

The absurdities that entertained Allenov are reminiscent, in their manifest "visibilities," of the names and images of "enemies of the state" that were blacked out in books and photographs in the 1930s (King 1997). By their sheer presence, the blacked-out passages and images screamed out what the System tried to hide: that people were disappearing, that history was being rewritten. Because such omissions and purges were evident and impossible to hide, a special kind of citizen had to be raised, one who did not see, did not trust the obvious. "The habit of holding the patently abnormal as normal" (Allenov 2003, p. 31)—of looking without seeing and of seeing what is not there, of letting someone else control and measure out what one should see and hear—was actively encouraged by the State. The newly infantilized observer should learn to see what he was meant to see and at the same time mistrust both reason (the ability to analyze) and his or her own senses, including the most important of them: the faculty of vision.

The whole System was based on visual *illiteracy* of a certain kind: the inability to read and analyze details or to trust one's own sensibility and sensuality. Another type of visual perception was actively encouraged: the ability to see the overall picture, become overwhelmed by its sheer opulence or apparent truth, and extract the one and only possible meaning.

It is important to point out here that this type of inattentive visual perception of major spectacles and official rituals went hand in hand with a meagerness, almost a sterility of visuality in private life. There is a strange paradox here as well. For contemporary Russian intellectuals, especially those older than forty, the words "beautiful" and "visually exciting" seem to belong to either Stalin's times or to the world of glossy magazines and the newly rich. It is this that Fridkes was referring to in the passage I quoted earlier. Some even find the concept of everyday beauty disgusting or ridiculous because, so they would say, it has no connection with their everyday life. But in this everyday life, the life that they oppose so vigorously to the world of "New Russians," they themselves seem to be still living in the visual environment of Soviet times.

Collectivization and the de-privatization (see Kruglova 2005, p. 98; Boim 2002) of everyday life, together with the almost total effacing of everything connected with the notion of coziness and comfort (Dashkova 2001, 2002), was effected in the 1920s and 1930s for the purpose of making a new man, one who could do without family, without home, and even without his own voice—a new man who would become "an empty vessel for storing depersonalised signs and norms" (Kruglova 2005, p. 121). To overcome the fear of repression, such a "new person" had to erase everything personal—and especially the outer, visual manifestations of the self. This in turn gave birth to communal flats, constructed in the 1920s and 1930s, where "for 38 rooms there was only one loo" [those are words from a song by Vladimir Vysotskii (Vysotskii 1975]. The notion of "impersonal living space" later transformed into standardized furniture from the 1960s through the 1980s, when almost every household possessed identical sets, called *stenka*, which were often very inconvenient and ugly, and so were, for example, armchairs in Soviet planes, such as the TU-154, which are still used. Those seats are too small and narrow to be comfortable—and not extremely visually attractive.

We may have gotten rid of many Soviet ideas but simple things, such as furniture or wallpaper, still influence our perception and often dominate our visual environment. The Russian photographer Vladimir Mishukov made a project called *The Family Cult* (Mishukov 2006) about modern Russian families; his photographs show the same sets of furniture produced twenty or thirty years ago. The *stenka* furniture appears in almost every photograph, whether it is the family of a street cleaner or of a deputy in parliament. I remember my own first experiences of life abroad (in London in 1993, in Helsinki in 1995): I was struck above all by the loving and personal attitude my Western friends, people of the same intellectual and professional background as mine, had to the inner spaces of their houses and apartments. There was a vividness of personal visual imagination and rich variety of images in their everyday living spaces and experiences.

3

There is vast literature on the ties between perception and ideology, and I will not repeat its conclusions here.[10] My main aim has been to show that the problem of the "inattentive observer" that is often discussed in books and articles on social realism, Soviet art, and everyday life in Russia has, in fact, much deeper roots in Russian culture and history. In 1917 ideology was born from the clash of the society as yet using traditionalist forms of perception and the "alien" culture of "modernity" for which there were no specifically developed tools of perception and analysis. Today, the situation seems to repeat itself again: maybe this time the "inattentive observer" might be able to learn how to become attentive. It is this that we have to deal with when it comes to deciding what visual literacy and visual studies should mean for modern Russia. It is a very serious problem for a society that has not yet developed a certain level of individual visual competence based on the ability to rationalize and perceive details—a society in which attention to such things has been not merely discouraged but at times severely repressed.

Nowadays we live in a country that, after the collapse of communism, was immediately exposed to a heavy bombing of fantastic and surreal advertising and commercial images. Consumer products and political party images from cultures with very different histories and very different attitudes to the visual rained down on us. They were as odd to us as Villiard de Honnecourt's heraldic lions or the images of sixteenth-century locusts. Visual literacy, I think, is necessarily based on certain common theories and social constructs, but it needs also to be deeply rooted in history because for Russians it also has a distinct national flavor.

References

Allenov, M. (2003), "'Ochevidnosti sistemnogo absurdizma skvoz' emblematiku moskovskogo metro." In: *Teksty o Tekstakh*, Moscow: Novoe Literaturnoe Obozrenie, pp. 8–102.

Besstuzhev-Riumin, K. N. ed. (1893), "Stateinyi spisok poslannika Grigoriia Mikulina i pod'iachego Ivana Zinov'eva v bytnost' ikh v Anglii." In: *Sbornik imperatorskogo russkogo istoricheskogo obshestva*, Vol. 37, St. Petersburg: XXXXX, pp. 315–363.

Boim, S. (2002), *Obshie mesta: Mifologiia povsednevnoi zhizni*, Moscow: Novoe Literaturnoe Obozrenie, 2002.

Dashkova, T. (2001), "'Rabotnitsu – v Massy': Politka sotsial'nogo modelirovaniia v sovetskikh zhenskikh zhurnalakh 1930-h godov." In: *Novoe Literaturnoe Obozrenie*, Vol. 50, 184–192.

Dashkova, T. (2002), "Ideologiia v litsakh: Formirovanie vizual'nogo kanona v sovetskikh zhenskikh zhurnalakh 1920-1930 godov." In: K. Aimermakher et al. (eds.), *Kul'tura i vlast' v usloviiakh kommunikativnoi revolutsii XX veka*, Moscow: AIRO-XX , pp. 103–128.

Epstein, M. (1991), "Ideologiia i iazyk: postroenie modeli i osmyslenie diskursa," *Voprosy iazykoznaniia*, 6, pp.19–33.

First Moscow Biennale of Contemporary Art (2005), http://www.moscowbiennale.ru/ru/. Accessed 26.10.2009..

Gombrich, E. H. (1989), "Truth and the Stereotype." In: *Art and Illusion: A Study in the Psychology of Pictorial Representation,* 9 ed. Princeton: Princeton University Press, pp. 63–90. First published in 1960; based on Gombrich's Mellon lectures given in Washington in 1956.

Giuntera, Khansa & Dobrenko, Evgeniia (2000), *Sotsrealisticheskii kanon*, St. Petersburg: Gumanitarnoe Agentstvo "Akademicheskiĭ Proekt."

Gudzy, N. K. (1970), "Beginning of the Russian Theater and Russian Dramaturgy," In: *History of Early Russian Literature*. Translated from Russian by Susan Wilbur Jones, New York: Octagon Books, 515–529.

Hodgen, Margaret Trabue (1964), *Early Anthropology in the Sixteenth and Seventeenth Centuries*, Philadelphia: University of Pennsylvania Press.

Kandinskii Prize (XXXX), http://www.kandinsky-prize.ru/en. Accessed 26.10.2009.

Khoruzhii, S. S. (1991), Diptikh bezmolviia: Asketicheskoe uchenie o cheloveke v bogoslovskom i filosofskom osveshenii. Moscow: Tsentr Psikhologii I Psikhoterapii.

Khoruzhii. S. S. (1994), *Posle pereryva: Puti russkoi filosofii*, Moscow: Izd-vo "Aleteiia."

King, D. (1997), *The Commissar Vanishes: The Falsification of Photographs and Art in Stalin's Russia*, New York: Metropolitan Books.

Kotliarchuk, A. S. (1995), "Ofitsialnye Prazdnichnye Tseremonii Velikorusskogo Goroda XVI-XVII vekov." In: *Problemy Sotsialnoi Istorii Europy ot Antichnosti do Novogo Vremeni*, Br'ansk: BGPU, pp.56–69.

Kruglova, T. (2005), Sovetskaia Hudozhestvennost' ili Neskromnoe Obaianie Sotsrealizma, Ekaterinburg: Izdatel'stvo Gumanitarnogo Universiteta.

Likhachev, D. S. (1947), *Russkie letopisi i ikh kulturno-istoricheskoe znachenie*, Moscow: Izd-vo Akademii nauk SSSR.

Likhachev, D. S. (1970), *Chelovek v literature Drevnei Rusi*, Moscow: Nauka.

Lotman, Iu.M. (1992), "O poniatii geograficheskogo prostranstva v russkikh srednevekovykh tekstakh." In: Iu.M. Lotman, *Izbrannye stat'i v trekh tomakh*, Vol. 2, Moscow, Aleksandra pp. 407–412.

Mishukov, V. (2006), *The Family Cult*. [Photography]. CEH Manej Central Exhibition Hall, Moscow.

Musvik, Viktoria (2002), "'And the King of Barbary's envoy had to stand in the yard': The perception of Elizabethan court festivals in Russia at the beginning of the seventeeth century." In: J. R. Mulryne, and E. Goldring (eds.), *Court Festivals of the*

European Renaissance: Art, politics and performance, Aldershot and Burlington: Ashgate Publishing, pp. 225–242.

Musvik, Viktoria (2008), "Interview with Vladimir Fridkes," http://www.fotonovosti.ru/content/arts_one/6/1972. Accessed 2 October 2008.

Robin, Régine (1992), *Socialist Realism: An Impossible Aesthetic*. Translated by Catherine Porter, Stanford: Stanford University Press.

Rogozhin, Nikolai (1994), "The ambassadorial book on the ties between Russia and England 1613-1614 as a historical source." In: Maija Jansson and Nikolai Rogozhin (eds.) and translated by Paul Bushkovitch, *England and the North: The Russian Embassy of 1613-1614*, Philadelphia: American Philosophical Society.

Strong, R. (1977), *The Cult of Elizabeth: Elizabethan Portraiture and Pageantry*, London: Thames and Hudson.

Uspenskii, Boris Anreevich (1994), "Dualisticheskii kharakter srednevekovoi russkoi kul'tury (na materiale 'Khozhdeniia za tri moria' Afanasiia Nikitina)." In: Boris Anreevich Uspenskii, *Izbrannye trudy*, Vol. 1, Moscow: Gnozis, pp. 110–218.

Vysotskii, Vladimir (1975), *Ballada o detstve,* http://vysotskiy.lit-info.ru/vysotskiy/stihi/626.htm. Accessed 5.11.2009.

Endnotes

1. Notice, for instance, vast literature on the tradition of Hesychasm in the Orthodox church. To see the Divine light, an Hesychast should stop registering information from his outer senses (including that of vision) and retire "inside himself," pray, look inwardly, and maintain inner stillness. Through such practices he would enclose the bodiless Energy of God, see the ideal transparent light, and find God's Kingdom inside himself. Not unlike yoga, the practice may involve certain breathing procedures and body postures, but the emphasis is always on prayer and the spiritual control over the mind and senses. See, for example, Sergei Khoruzhiii (1991, 1994) and other works by the same author and texts by Pavel Florenskii and Vladimir Losskii.

2. *Action Half Life* was a photography project done in 2003-2005 by one of the most well-known Russian art groups AES+F. It imitated the computer game with the same name.

3. The term "inattentive observer" is from Allenov (2003).

4. With "too little," "too much," and "enough" in invisible scare quotes: all these subjects are matters of perspective; I take that as a given in this project.

5. This passage refers to the first Kandinsky prize (2007), before the second Kandinsky Prize (2008) named its winner. The winner for 2008 was announced on December 10, 2008. Alexey Belyaev-Gintovt is well-known in Russia for his support of the group "Euroasian Youth Union" that names among its idols Ivan the Terrible and Joseph Stalin. Belyaev-Gintovt is also noted for his ultra-right views and love for totalitarian art. Even his inclusion in the 2008 shortlist created a huge controversy; when Belyaev-Gintovt's name was announced at the 2008 award ceremony one of the previous year's nominees, Anatolii Osmolovskii, cried out: "Disgrace!"

6. I am drawing here on my article Musvik (2002).

7. In the sixteenth century, such documents typically took the form of a very detailed written account of the visit, made on the basis of a journal or diary that the diplomat was ordered to write on the spot, day by day, without adding or forgetting anything. On return, after checking by the Ambassadorial Department or the Foreign Office [*Posol'skii prikaz*], the document would be presented to the Tsar and later, with other documents relating to the embassy, would be bound into so-called ambassadorial books [*posol'skie knigi*] (see Rogozhin 1994). At the time there was no difference between official diplomatic accounts and literary descriptions of foreign climes; *stateinye spiski* had the features of both genres.

8. When, in 1606, during the Times of Trouble, the Tsar known as "False Dmitry I" tried to introduce into Russian court culture triumphal arches and fireworks, onlookers referred to the effect as a "diabolical performance" [*besovskoe igralishche*]. (Kotliarchuk 1995, p. 60)

9. When this article had already been written many people in Russia were shocked and outraged by the news that during the restoration of another metro station (Kurskaia) the lines from the Soviet anthem "We were raised by Stalin" were returned to the station's wall. After the complaints the officials explained that it was all done in the name of "authenticity" and that the station had been given back its "historical look." However the lines about "the great Lenin who has illuminated our way" that had once been there were no longer on the wall after the restoration. The press asked if Stalin's name was now more dear to the hearts of certain Metro officials than Lenin's. In a few weeks time, Lenin's name was also returned to the station's walls.

10. See, for instance, the cited works by Kruglova (2005) and Allenov (2003), also Robin (1992), Giuntera and Dobrenko (2000), and Epstein (1991).

CRITICAL RESPONSE

Esther Sánchez-Pardo

In his "Theses on the Philosophy of History" (1940) Walter Benjamin writes about the task of the historian and about the new relation between past and present that is registered in the form of images. "The past can be seized only as an image which flashes up at the instant when it can be recognized and is never seen again" (Benjamin 1992a, p. 247). History is no longer a narrative of teleological progress, and the way in which the present *lives* the past takes the form of fragmentary flashes or image traces. Any such image "not recognized by the present as one of its own concerns threatens to disappear irretrievably" (Benjamin 1992a, p. 247). Dislodged from the continuum of time, the image is that which resists narrative resolution and interrupts its logic. Images hold the possibility of messianic redemption precisely because they cannot be co-opted into a narrative of historical progress grounded in "homogeneous, empty time" (Benjamin 1992a, p. 253). The past as envisaged by Paul Klee's *Angelus Novus* (1920; Israel Museum, Jerusalem) is a single, catastrophic wreckage of fragments blowing the Angel of History "into the future to which its back is turned," is a past that refuses to be made transparent (Benjamin 1992a, p. 238).

Well before the "Theses on the Philosophy of History," in *The Origin of German Tragic Drama*, Benjamin had put forward his theory of allegory. Allegory, he wrote, comes into being once the written sign fails to find meaning fulfilled in itself: "The result is that nature, far from an organic whole, appears in arbitrary arrangements, as a lifeless, fragmentary, untidy clutter of emblems. The coherence of language is similarly shattered . . . Allegorists, like alchemists, hold dominion over an infinite transformation of meanings, in contrast to the one, true word of God" (Benjamin 1996, p. 173).

All these fragments are "emblematic," and the shattering of linguistic coherence emerges out of the unprecedented proliferation of signs found in Baroque culture. Language turned opaque, having lost its accustomed transparency of meaning, is registered in the image. The visual sign is now privileged. As Benjamin argues, "With every idea the moment of expression coincides with a veritable eruption of images, which give rise to a chaotic mass of metaphors" (Benjamin 1996, p. 173). And the operation of allegory involves "a 'crossing of the borders of a different mode,' an advance of the plastic arts into the territory of the 'rhetorical' arts" (Benjamin 1996, p. 177). This thesis, of a border crossing into the visual, encompasses a wide range of practices and has gained momentum in the rhetoric of recent critical theory.[1]

That we live today in a culture "overwhelmingly dominated by the visual and the image" seems a far too obvious fact of today's existence, but the expansion of culture and its greater diffusion throughout the social, as Fredric Jameson has warned us, produces effects whose implications are extremely complex and difficult to assess (Jameson 1998, p. 100). In Jameson's view, in postmodernism "the very space of culture itself has expanded, becoming coterminous with market society in such a way that the cultural is no longer limited to its earlier, traditional, or experimental forms, but is consumed throughout daily life itself, in shopping, in professional activities, in the various often televisual forms of leisure, in production for the market and in the consumption of those market products, indeed, in the most secret folds and corners of the quotidian. Social space is now saturated with the culture of the image" (Jameson 1998, p. 111).

In a previous era, art was a realm beyond commodification, but as Jameson grimly remarks, in postmodernity, all forms of art, high and low, everything in the sphere of culture along with image production itself have been absorbed by the market, and "the image is the commodity today, and this is why it is vain to expect a negation of the logic of commodity production from it" (Jameson 1998, p. 135). In other words, there seems to be no room for resistance within the realm of the image: an indiscriminate bombardment of images excludes creative agency, disavows the recourse to utopia, and leaves the individual at the mercy of a particular mediatic technology.[2]

This, at least, is how I would theorize the pairing of the visual and verbal that is employed by the authors of this book. Benjamin's critique throws a different light on it: the visual appears, in his account, at the twilight of the transparency of language. Jameson's account is an eloquent warning of the pervasiveness of the visual, and its complicity with capitalism. These, I think, are the signposts of the territory that this book has sought to explore.

I will respond in two directions: first, a brief meditation on Homi Bhabha's idea that the discourse of the novel and the newspaper—two principal vehicles of literacy in nation states—takes place in a posited "future perfect," rather than in a present, and second, an equally brief exploration of the possibility that the visual comprises a site of violence and resistance, in addition to its ubiquitous commodification.

The novel and the newspaper as a future tense

In addressing the question of whether some cultures are more visual than others, one should discriminate between culture and nation and know that there is a trend that seems to equate unproblematically a certain culture with a certain nation. In any event, for practical reasons, discussions of the visual in different cultures are associated in this book with modern nations (Slovenia, Japan, Ireland, Poland, China, Russia) and here I will be addressing the role of the visual in the domain of the nation, bearing in mind both a larger cultural context and the current processes of globalization.

As Benedict Anderson proposed in his classic *Imagined Communities*, "The nation is an imagined political community, and imagined as both inherently limited and sovereign. It is imagined because the members of even the smallest nation will never know most of his fellow-members, meet them, or even hear of them, yet in the minds of each lives the image of their communion" (Anderson 1991, p. 4). And in Anderson's view, all communities are to be distinguished by the style in which they are imagined. Anderson expands on the cultural roots of nationalism and his rhetoric exhibits an emphasis on images, on imagining, and on the realm of the visual. "Ghostly national imaginings" are a common feature of nations, Anderson says; in such imaginings death, immortality, and their connection to regeneration (the yet unborn) are crucial (Anderson 1991, p. 9).

Those imagined communities of nations did replace religious communities and dynastic realms in the wake of a fundamental change produced in "modes of apprehending the world" (Anderson 1991, p. 22). Anderson goes back to the visual representations of sacred communities in the religious art of medieval churches and in the paintings of the early Italian and Flemish masters. A reality that was eminently visual and aural—the sermon—was a powerful pedagogic resource in the hands of the Latin-reading clerisy, and it fulfilled an ideological function in the social and moral upbringing of the illiterate masses.

In the eighteenth century, the novel and the newspaper came to be the privileged means for representing the "kind of imagined community that is the nation" (Anderson 1991, p. 25). The novel proved invaluable for the representation of simultaneous actions in what Anderson calls "homogeneous, empty time." Both the novel and the newspaper are mass-produced industrial commodities and with their dissemination the imagined world came to be visibly rooted in everyday life. This was the onset of Benjamin's "age of mechanical reproduction," and it all owed its success to print capitalism, whose initial market was literate Europe. In Anderson's view, the convergence of capitalism and print technology with the rise of print languages laid the bases for national consciousness and created the possibility of "a new form of imagined community, which in its basic morphology set the stage for the modern nation" (Anderson 1991, p. 46).

In other words, members of a nation can only perceive the nation as a whole by referring to the image of it that they have construed in their own minds. Problematic as it may seem for the definition of the nation, the emphasis on the image, on shared images and feelings (belongingness, fraternity), raises the question of how individuals come to construct the image of the nation to which they belong. A large set of variables plays a role here, from religion and language to geography, colonial policies, and the like. It would be interesting to investigate whether these repertoires of images share common ground and if they do, the definition of nation, and by extension of culture, should emphasize them as a common denominator. The importance and the scope of the visual in a specific culture is never the product of an individual or a group of individuals but rather of a "visual" community with a historical specificity.[3]

Against Anderson's premise that "homogeneous, empty time" is real, Bhabha's response in *DissemiNation: Time, Narrative, and the Margins of the Modern Nation* explores the fractures and fissures in Anderson's imagined community. He counters Anderson's narrative with diasporic double writing, the dissemination of peoples that cannot be accounted for in imagined communities. Instead, Bhabha seeks to examine "the complex strategies of cultural identification and discursive address that function in the name of 'the people' and make them the immanent subjects and objects of a range of social and literary narratives" (Bhabha 1990, p. 292).

Bhabha's project seeks to account for the fractures that run through the social body without occluding irreducible difference. The available strategies for narrating the nation belie its own liminality.[4] Bhabha makes clear that the narrative of a historically linear nationhood sustains itself by a forced repression of other narratives that might disrupt its hegemony.[5] Bhabha posits another time of writing, namely, the future perfect. In his view, "The symbolic historicity of the national culture is inscribed in the strange temporality of the future perfect . . . in such a historical time, the deeply repressed past initiates a strategy of repetition that disturbs sociological totalities within which we recognize the modernity of the national culture" (Bhabha 1990, p. 303–304). The future perfect becomes thus the time of the nation, the time of the migrants, margins, and minorities.[6] This, we might suggest, offers an articulation of desiring belonging as "future," a desire that can be spoken in the future perfect.

The image as violence

The construction of an ancient national history in the vernacular produces a homogeneous totality. Arguably, this functions as the realist novel Bhabha critiques (Bhabha 1990, pp. 308–309). This impossible unison is frustrated both at the level of narrative and at the level of language. Anderson, Bhabha argues, "misses the alienating and iterative time of the sign" (Bhabha 1990, p. 309). In *Imagined Communities* (Anderson 1991), he assumes that vernacular languages, the rise of which precedes nationalism, are uniformly familiar for all speakers. According to Bhabha, Anderson's narrative cannot account for the multiple ways in which language is foreign to all its speakers, both indigenous and migrant. And differences exist not only outside a nation or outside of a language group but also within. Certainly, a nation requires foreigners outside its borders for its continued intelligibility; however, Bhabha is interested in what happens on the inside of the borders, at the margins of the nation. He locates an otherness within the people-as-one (Bhabha 1990, p. 301). At the margins and in minorities and migrants, Bhabha finds the transformative potential of the supplement. It is not that the margins need to be brought to the center in an inclusionary politics but rather, the belatedness, the secondariness of the supplement iteratively transforms not just the social body but the national narrative. Margins and minorities cannot be imagined by the national narrative, the metaphor of the many in the one, but are constitutive of a "nation" that is iterative. The iterations reconfigure pedagogical and performative time, neither of which can be viewed as static or fixed in some stable, knowable past.

The visual can also be understood as a form of violence in its own right. Margins and minorities cannot be thus imagined, perceived, or apprehended: they are proscribed from representation. Whenever images from the margins do appear, the violence of representation shows them as produced to maintain the hegemonic pattern of dominance, as radically Other.

It is my contention that we should also talk about counter-images of the nation (culture) as part of a movement of resistance to homogenization and commodification. The best examples I know are the work of Brazilian photographer Sebastião Salgado[7] and of the Vietnamese-born filmmaker Trinh T. Minh-Ha.[8]

And we can extend Bhabha's argument by recourse to Roland Barthes's idea of the punctum in *Camera Lucida*.[9] The singularity of the punctum attends to the image in subtle ways, and Barthes associates the punctum with the movement of the look beyond the frame or picture of what is given to be seen to what lies outside. The eye can always look from a position that is not assigned in advance and affirm certain marginal elements at the expense of those that are valorized in a certain culture. The punctum is a detail that produces in the spectator a major obstacle to verbalization and an operation of "exemption from meaning."[10] And Barthes shocks us with the possibility of apprehending the image from a singular and unexpected vantage point.

Whether we theorize using the punctum or the visual proscription of minorities, the visual appears as a potential act of violence, one situated, again potentially, in the present tense—and therefore an ideologically charged counter-movement to the "future perfect" of literacy. For me, the authors in this book take insufficient notice of this philosophic, or rather temporal, difference, particularly when they portray the visual and verbal as equal, comparable, contrasting, or merely different.

Problems of writing about "visual cultures"

So how do we open up the visual to the discussion of cultural differences? What is at stake in choosing a specific culture to be observed and under whose eyes (Japan in Barthes's *Empire of Signs* (Barthes 1983), and the allure of an adopted culture for a foreign analyst, as Manghani's and Van Heuckelom's essays prove)? In what ways should we talk of visual communities that escape the boundaries of the nation?

We might draw an analogy between what is going on in the domain of visual and that of literary studies. As Wai Chee Dimock has persuasively argued: "We need to stop thinking of national literatures as the linguistic equivalents of territorial maps . . . the nation state is not all, that when it comes to the extended life of literary objects, the inscriptional power of the state is not complete . . . An emerging and globalizing readership undermines it on both fronts. Theorized as the consequences of this global readership, literature handily outlives the finite scope of the nation. It brings into play a different set of temporal and spatial coordinates. It urges on us the entire planet as a unit of analysis" (Dimock 2001). And it is as well a symptom of our times that the global visual has become hegemonic with the decline of readers and print culture.

As the essays in this book demonstrate, this does not mean that the visual has not been traditionally repressed—to the contrary. Is the visual preeminent because it is more difficult to capture? Or because, as Benjamin says, it emerges in the era of allegory, with the growing opacity of language? Or, as Bhabha claims against Anderson, that literary imagination is in a future tense? These questions have to be asked, in each instance, before the chronicling of the visual and verbal can begin.

In general terms, the resistance of the visual to narrativization makes it much harder to incorporate into a teleologically oriented frame. As Luke Gibbons shrewdly writes in support of his thesis about the sublime in Irish culture and art, in many current instances of Irish "political" art—is there an art that is not political?—images seek to represent what cannot be seen. Landscape, for example, "is no longer scenery, a source of visual pleasure, but is a menacing presence, concealing as much as it reveals . . . To ask what is happening on the landscape is to narrativize it, to open it up to competing stories and interpretations of what happened," so that even the cityscape may become "a contested site of memory and denial" (Gibbons 2009).

Possible ways forward

I believe we should insist on the historicity of the seeing subject, and this might probably enable the forging of a certain visual critical agency, aware of its limitations and refusing any totalizing and privileged perspective. We need to provide more diachronic surveys of visuality to examine historical ways of seeing that are now only accessible through representation and discourse, ways that could delineate a trajectory of the conditions of perceiving and codes of depicting, ultimately throwing light on how these conditions correspond to subject positions and power relations in society. An effort has been made in the case studies collected in this book.

Today, global forces impinge on the old cultural boundaries and disable the concepts of situatedness, boundedness, and community. We can probably talk of the collapse of the idea of "imagined communities." To what extent would visual communities hold as such in today's fragmented, nomad, late-capitalist world where sophisticated and highly technified modes of production draw an insurmountable line between transnational corporations and workers—who are no longer nationals of a country but rather part of an exploited and displaced labor force? In what ways can we talk of diasporic cultures that struggle to gain access to visibility and, ultimately, to the visual, aside from the paradigm of the impoverished and dispossessed members of a new global class?

According to Arjun Appadurai, the new media and mass migration have had a joint effect on the work of the imagination as a constitutive feature of modern subjectivity, producing a new order of instability. Because viewers and images are in simultaneous circulation, they create irregularities that do not fit into circuits easily bound within local, national, or regional spaces. There is clear evidence that consumption of mass media throughout the world often provokes resistance, irony, selectivity, and, in general, agency (Appadurai 2002, pp. 174, 176). All this on the positive side.

Yet, the writers in this book all participate in a kind of linguistic colonialism, where English has become the creole of the world to discuss the implications of transnationality upon culture, language, and power. And the sorts of communities we more typically consider "virtual" are those created on the Internet to which the majority of the educated citizens of the West belong.[11]

In the wake of Michel Foucault's panopticon and surveillance, Guy Debord's *Society of the Spectacle,* and Fredric Jameson's late-capitalist postmodern market society, I would also argue that an active resistance to looking may be the measure of our own desire for freedom [see Foucault (1995), Jameson (1991, 1992), and Debord (1994)]. This can be a mode of resistance to power, which is not yet freedom.

Is it possible to articulate this resistance to looking, to the look, in the context of the idea of the community, and in a sense that cannot be co-opted? Which parts of ourselves and of our communities can we retain and which parts would be appropriated?[12] As contemporary critical and visual theory has taught us, it is clear that we can think of strategies for actively looking but inversely, can we talk about strategies for resisting to look?

In "The Storyteller," Walter Benjamin attributed the demise of storytelling to the fact that "the communicability of experience is decreasing" (Benjamin 1992b, p. 86). This also holds true in a different way in the domain of the visual. The visual can no longer be rooted in the verities of the stable and ancient world of nations but rather of a world that has gone global and where the communicability of the visual cultural/national may as well have become unintelligible.

In considering these limitations, we should not underestimate the subversive power that invisibility entails. It may be the beginning of our way to freedom.

References

Anderson, Benedict (1991), *Imagined Communities: Reflections on the Origin and Spread of Nationalism*, London: Verso.

Appadurai, Arjun (2002), "Here and Now." In: Nicholas Mirzoeff (ed.), *Visual Culture Reader*, London: Routledge, pp. 173–179.

Aronowitz, S. & Giroux, H. (1991), *Postmodern Education: Politics, Culture and Social Criticism*, Minneapolis: University of Minnesota Press.

Barthes, Roland (1982), *Camera Lucida: Reflections on Photography*. Translated by Richard Howard. New York: Farrar, Straus and Giroux.

Barthes, Roland (1983), *Empire of Signs*. Translated from French by Richard Howard, London: Jonathan Cape.

Bhabha, Homi (1990), "DissemiNation: Time, narrative, and the margins of the modern nation." In: *Nation and Narration*, London: Routledge, 291–322.

Bhabha, Homi (1994), *The Location of Culture*, London: Routledge.

Benjamin, Walter (1992a), "Theses on the Philosophy of History." In: *Illuminations: Essays and Reflections*. Translated by Harry Zohn, London: Fontana, pp. 245–258.

Benjamin, Walter (1992b), "The Storyteller." In: *Illuminations: Essays and Reflections*. Translated by Harry Zohn, London: Fontana, pp. 83–107.

Benjamin, Walter (1996), *The Origin of German Tragic Drama*. Translated from German by John Osborne, London: Verso.

Bourdieau, Pierre (1990), *The Logic of Practice*. Translated from French by Richard Nice, Cambridge: Polity Press.

Debord, Guy (1994), *The Society of the Spectacle*. Translated from French by Donald Nicholson-Smith, New York: Zone Books.

Dimock, Wai Chee (2001), "Literature for the Planet," *PMLA* 116 (1), pp. 173–188.

Elkins, James (2003), *Visual Studies: A Skeptical Introduction*, London: Routledge.

Esrock, Ellen (1994), *The Reader's Eye: Visual Imaging as Reader Response*, Baltimore: Johns Hopkins University Press.

Fish, Stanley (1980), *Is There A Text in This Class? The Authority of Interpretive Communities*, Cambridge: Harvard University Press.

Foucault, Michel (1995), *Discipline and Punish: The Birth of the Prison*, New York: Vintage.

Gibbons, Luke (2009), "Words upon the Windowpane: Image, text, and Irish culture." In: James Elkins (ed.), *Visual Cultures*, Bristol: Intellect Books, pp. 46–61.

Jameson, Fredric (1991), *Postmodernism, or The Cultural Logic of Late Capitalism*, Durham: Duke University Press.

Jameson, Fredric (1992), *Signatures of the Visible*, London: Verso.

Jameson, Fredric (1998), "Transformations of the Image." In: *The Cultural Turn: Selected Writings on the Postmodern 1893–1998*, London: Verso, pp. 93–135.

Messaris, Paul (1994), *Visual Literacy: Image, Mind, and Reality*, Boulder: Westview Press.

Minh-Ha, Trinh T. (1982), *Reassemblage*. 40 mins, filmed in rural Senegal. Prod. Jean-Paul Bourdier.

Minh-Ha, Trinh T. (1985), *Naked Spaces: Living is Round*, 135 mins, filmed in West Africa. Prod. Jean-Paul Bourdier.

Minh-Ha, Trinh T. (1989), *Surname Viet Given Name Nam*, 108 mins, filmed in Vietnam and United States. Prod. Jean-Paul Bourdier.

Mitchell, W. J. T. (1994), *Picture Theory: Essays on Verbal and Visual Representation*, Chicago: University of Chicago Press.

Pratt, Mary Louise (1992), *Imperial Eyes: Travel Writing and Transculturation*, London: Routledge.

Salgado, Sebastião (1986), *Other Americas*, New York: Pantheon Books.

Salgado, Sebastião (1993), *Workers: An archaeology of the Industrial Age*, New York: Aperature.

Salgado, Sebastião (2000a), *The Children: Refugees and Migrants*, New York: Aperature.

Salgado, Sebastião (2000b), *Migrations: Humanity in Transition*, New York: Aperature.

Salgado, Sebastião (2004), *Sahel: The End of the Road*, Berkeley: University of California.

Endnotes

1. It would also be possible to frame our discussion of the visual in different cultures by rehearsing the rhetoric of the "contact zone," Mary Louise Pratt's felicitous metaphor for the social space "where disparate cultures meet, clash, and grapple with each other, often in highly asymmetrical relations of domination and subordination." Or in Bhabha's idea of "Third Space," where cultures intersect. He sees the space between different art practices and between different theories as "a very interesting place of enunciation," because it is an occasion for interruption and displacement—for rhetorical adjustment. The zone of mediation, according to Bhabha, may be theorized as the process of "cultural hybridity" giving rise to something new and initially unrecognizable, an area of "negotiation" of meaning and representation." Acknowledging the "Third Space" establishes grounds for questioning seemingly fixed and naturalized habits of critical response, and it promises an interesting vantage point for change and transformation [see Pratt (1992, p. 4) and Bhabha (1994, pp. 1–34)].

2. Among those of us who work in the ancient regime of print culture, one senses a common anxiety about the loss of print literacy in an increasingly visual world. In a scenario where visual learning is becoming dominant, and the media (television, film, the press) engage all audiences in the global village, the old textual paradigm appears outdated. Students are exposed to electronic media from the very early stages of education, and the domain of visual experience in a world dominated by sophisticated technologies of communication has become part of what Pierre Bourdieu calls "habitus." In *The Logic of Practice*, Bourdieu (1990) defines habitus as follows, "The conditionings associated with a particular class of conditions of existence produce habitus, systems of durable, transposable dispositions, structured structures predisposed to function as structuring structures, that is, as principles which generate and organize practices and representations that can be objectively adapted to their outcomes without presupposing a conscious aiming at ends or an express mastery of

the operations necessary in order to attain them" (Bourdieu 1990, p. 53).

Visual education should probably become a part of the curriculum both at school and at university level, and recent critics have argued in favor of the advantages that an emphasis on visual literacy would bring for the general public (See, among others, Aronowitz and Giroux 1991), Esrock (1994), Mitchell (1994), and Messaris (1994).

3. I suggest it would be worth investigating the analogy between what Stanley Fish (1980) called "interpretive communities" and what I am calling "visual communities." Fish defined them as follows, "It is interpretive communities, rather than either the text or the reader, that produce meanings and are responsible for the emergence of formal features. Interpretive communities are made up of those who share interpretive strategies not for reading but for writing texts, for constituting their properties. In other words these strategies exist prior to the act of reading and therefore determine the shape of what is read rather than, as is usually assumed, the other way around" (Fish 1980, p. 14). We might as well talk about visual communities that are made up of those who share strategies for producing not for consuming images but strategies that are prior to the act of looking and establishing a condition of "to be looked-atness" that determines what appears in the field of vision.

    Interestingly, in the essay Luke Gibbons included in this volume, he touches upon the interrelation between images and words and upon the way they construct meanings in a transformative process in which transmutation of images into words and words into images plays an important role in social dynamics. He writes, "[The] images are important, not just for what they show, but for the narratives they trigger in a community . . ." (Gibbons 2009, p. 56). Here Gibbons alludes to the construction of cultural memory in Ireland in the context of recent Irish visual art.

4. This idea of the liminality of the nation and of the liminality of the people is foregrounded and emphasis is placed on the margins not the totality: "It is a mark of the ambivalence of the nation as narrative strategy...that it produces a continual slippage into analogous, even metonymic, categories, like the people, minorities or 'cultural difference' that continually overlap in the act of writing the nation. What is displayed in this displacement and repetition of terms is the nation as the measure of the liminality of cultural modernity" (Bhabha 1990, p. 292).

5. The presence of the repressed described by Bhabha in terms of the Freudian uncanny resurfaces in oppositional practices of signification that are raced, classed, and gendered. This enables him to represent the national time–space as a "double time" in which the dominant national temporal narrative (the "pedagogical," in his words) is contested by the performance of "counternarratives of the nation that continually evoke and erase its totalizing boundaries" (Bhabha 1990, p. 300).

6. Finally, he sets out to find "the join," and at this point the search for rupture becomes in this moment at least, the desire for belonging: "To live in the unhomely world, to find its ambivalences and ambiguities enacted in the house of fiction, or its sundering and splitting performed in the work of art, is also to affirm a profound desire for social solidarity: 'I am looking for the join… I want to join … I want to join'" (Bhabha 1994, p. 18).

7. Salgado (1944–) has conducted five major projects: photographing the rural peasant in Latin America ("Other Americas"; Salgado 1986); the terrible African famine of 1984/85 ("Sahel"; Salgado 2004); and the situation of the manual laborer displaced in a society dominated by sophisticated technologies ("Workers"; Salgado 1993). His current work is concerned with the refugees, migrants, and dispossessed "(Migrations"; Salgado 2000b), and also with the children ("Children"; Salgado 2000a) who are victims of wars and crises.

8. Vietnamese-born Trinh T. Minh-Ha has explored different genres, all formally complex experiments from documentary and ethnographic film (*Reassemblage*; Minh-Ha 1982; *Naked Spaces*; Minh-Ha 1985) to films such as *Surname Viet Given Name Nam* (Minh-Ha 1989), where she is concerned with the role of Vietnamese women in history and the themes of dislocation and exile.

9. Barthes (1982) distinguishes between two looks, the "stadium" and the "punctum." He says that "the studium is "ultimately always coded. The punctum is not" (Barthes 1982, p. 51). The punctum is that "prick" experienced by the subject when he or she directs his or her look away from those elements in an image that speak with the "voice" of "knowledge" and "culture" (Barthes 1982, p. 51).

10. James Elkins (2003) finds in Barthes's notion of the punctum a "succinct critique of visual studies *avant la lettre*." In Elkins's view, "the punctum, stands for Barthes as any kind of seeing that is personal, embodied and unpredictable. Ultimately the experience of the punctum is the entire point of attending to images in the first place" (Elkins 2003, p. 193). For Barthes, this exemption from meaning is analogous to the satori of Zen, "A detail overwhelms the entirety of my reading; it is an intense mutation of my interest, a fulguration. By the mark of something, the photograph is no longer 'anything whatever.' This something has triggered me, has provoked a tiny shock, a satori, the passage of a void (it is of no importance that is referent is insignificant" (Elkins 2003, p. 49).

11. At present, as new forms of consciousness (national, cultural, or otherwise) emerge out of new technologies, new kinds of images struggle to create new kinds of subjects. The main technological basis for the emergence of the transnational virtual

community is the global network of computers. Just as Anderson demonstrated, print capitalism was important for the creation of imagined communities that would evolve into nations; today, we might suggest that electronic capitalism is the necessary environment for the development of a transnation.

12. And how can we theorize a space for secrecy, privacy, intimacy—a space resistant to surveillance? Emancipatory practices do have to do with political creativity and survival.

Contributors

James Elkins teaches at the School of the Art Institute of Chicago and is director of Events and Publications at University College Cork, Ireland. His most recent books include *Six Stories from the End of Representation: Images in Painting, Photography, Astronomy, Microscopy, Particle Physics, and Quantum Mechanics, 1980–2000* (Stanford University Press 2008), the edited volumes *Re-Enchantment* (Routledge 2008), co-edited with David Morgan; *Renaissance Theory* (Routledge 2008), co-edited with Robert Williams; and *Landscape Theory* (Routledge 2007), co-edited with Rachael DeLue (mail@imagehistory.org)

Luke Gibbons is Professor in Irish Literary and Cultural Studies at the National University of Ireland, Maynooth. His most recent book is *Gaelic Gothic: Race, Colonialism and Irish Culture* (Arlen House 2004); his *Edmund Burke and Ireland: Aesthetics, Politics and the Colonial Sublime, 1750–1850* (Cambridge University Press) was published in 2003. His other books include *The Quiet Man* (Cork University Press 2002); *Transformations in Irish Culture* (Cork University Press 1996), and (with Kevin Rockett and John Hill) *Cinema in Ireland* (Syracuse University Press 1988). He is currently preparing *Joyce's Ghosts: Modernism, Memory and Colonial Ireland.*

Sunil Manghani is a lecturer in the School of Arts at York St. John's University. He is co-editor, with Jon Simons and Adrian Piper, of *Images: A Reader*, a comprehensive survey of texts on visuality (Sage Publications 2006); "Picturing Berlin: Piecing Together a Public Sphere," *Invisible Culture: An Electronic Journal for Visual Culture* (http://www. Rochester.edu 2003); and "Experimental Text-Image Travel Literature," *Theory, Culture, & Society* (Sage Publications 2003). (s.manghani@yorksj.ac.uk)

Viktoria Musvik teaches in the Philological Department at Moscow State University, Lomonosov, Russia. Her specialty is the dissemination of visual culture studies in Russia.

Ding Ning teaches in the Department of Art Studies at Peking University. His publications include *Dimensions of Reception* (Tianjin 1990), *Psychology of the Visual Arts* (Harbin 1994), *Dimensions of Duration: Toward a Philosophy of Art History* (Beijing 1997*), Depth of Art* (Hangzhou 1999), *Fifteen Lectures on Western Art History* (Beijing 2003), and *Spectrum of Images: Toward a Cultural Dimension of Visual Arts* (Beijing 2005)—all in Chinese. (Address: 5-304 Lanqiyingxiaoqu, Chengfu Rd., Haidian District, Beijing 100084, China; dingning@pku.edu.cn)

Esther Sánchez-Pardo is an associate professor of English at Complutense University in Madrid, Spain. She works on Modernism and is interested in the intersection of literature, psychoanalysis, and the visual arts. She recently published *Cultures of the Death Drive: Melanie Klein and Modernist Melancholia* (Duke University Press 2003). She is coauthor of *Ophelia's Legacy: Schizotexts in Twentieth Century Women's Literature* (Horas y Horas 2001, in Spanish) and has coedited *Women, Identities and Poetry: Contemporary Poets of the United States and Canada* (Horas y Horas 1999, in Spanish) and *Feeling the Worlds* (Huerga & Fierro 2001, in Spanish). (esanchez_pardo@filol.ucm.es)

Andrej Smrekar was Director of the Narodna Galerija (National Gallery) in Ljubljana, Slovenia through 2005 and serves as keeper of works of art on paper. He is a specialist on Slovenian Modernist painting and the author of studies on Slovene artists Rihard Jakopič, Ivan Grohar and Marjan Pogačnik.

Kris Van Heuckelom is an assistant professor of Polish Language and Literature in the Department of Oriental and Slavic Studies, Faculty of Arts, at Katholieke Universiteit Leuven. His most recent book is *(Un)masking Bruno Schulz. New Combinations, Further Fragmentations, Ultimate Reintegrations.* (Rodopi 2009, coedited with Dieter De Bruyn). Other books include *Perspectives on Slavic Literatures* (Rodopi 2005, coedited with David Danaher) and *Looking at Light Reflected by Earth. Visuality in the Poetry of Czesław Miłosz* (Polish Academy of Sciences 2004, in Polish) (kris@vanheuckelom.be).